Style: An Anti-Textbook

STYLE: AN ANTI-TEXTBOOK

Richard A. Lanham

New Haven and London, Yale University Press, 1974

Copyright © 1974 by Yale University.
All rights reserved. This book may not be
reproduced, in whole or in part, in any form
(except by reviewers for the public press),
without written permission from the publishers.
Library of Congress catalog card number: 73-86906
International standard book number: 0-300-01720-0

Designed by John O. C. McCrillis
and set in Baskerville type.
Printed in the United States of America by
The Colonial Press, Inc., Clinton, Massachusetts

Published in Great Britain, Europe, and Africa by
Yale University Press, Ltd., London.
Distributed in Latin America by Kaiman & Polon,
Inc., New York City; in Australasia and Southeast
Asia by John Wiley & Sons Australasia Pty. Ltd.,
Sydney; in India by UBS Publishers' Distributors Pvt.,
Ltd., Delhi; in Japan by John Weatherhill, Inc., Tokyo.

For Carol

And the things thought essential to a textbook-impersonality, numbered and labeled paragraphs, an obvious style, test questions at the end of the chapter—are they not death? The Dark Ages, it seems, was a time when people read text-books and thought they were literature.

Charles Horton Cooley, *Life and the Student*

Contents

Preface   ix

1   The Problem and "The Books"   1

2   The Uses of Obscurity   21

3   The Opaque Style   44

4   The Delights of Jargon   69

5   Poetic Prose   94

6   Essential Hypocrisies   115

7   The Ultimate Morality of Mind   125

Bibliographical Note   136

Preface

A word about subject and audience. This book seeks to provide both a preface to the study of prose composition and a context for it. It argues that the premises from which the study of composition now departs—clarity, plainness, sincerity—are incomplete and seriously misleading. It suggests alternative premises and an alternative pedagogy, and is thus about both prose style and the teaching of prose style, addressed to both student and teacher. It also suggests that the study of style has objectives more profound, and more enjoyable, than simply the faithful and useful communication of concepts. It seeks to supply, that is, new purposes for stylistic study as well as new premises.

This is not a textbook, then, but a counterstatement to the textbooks now in use and the widespread attitudes they express. It is neither a practical guide to better prose, a handbook of do's and don'ts, nor a scholarly analysis, historical or schematic, of prose styles. It aims, rather, to provide a framework within which such books can be studied with more profit than now they are.

I have tried to reach not only the classroom but a general American audience, for the problem extends beyond the classroom to the nation. The specifically American setting is crucial and nothing but confusion has ever come from ignoring it. America is the only country in the world rich enough to have the leisure, and democratic enough to have the inclination, to teach its whole citizenry not merely to write, but to write well. Time will try the truth of this hopeful enterprise. Meanwhile, such a purpose seems new enough, and daring enough, to require premises, pedagogy, and purposes equally so.

My colleague and friend, Alan Roper, has given the typescript that kind of critical reading and sympathetic

understanding every author dreams of, especially when his
doubts are greatest and his hopes about to expire. I would
also like to thank Stanley E. Fish, Ronald Freeman, Mary
R. Georges, Ruth M. Holmes, Loren G. Lee, and James
Carbone, for helpful readings and suggestions. And I stand
in debt to a yet larger group, my students: those in English
1 and 2, and in the remedial sections, at Dartmouth; those
in Composition for High School Teachers, in Advanced
Composition, and in English 1 and 2, at UCLA; and those
students in my upper division and graduate classes, who did
not know they had signed on for a composition class too, but
did not resent the addition so much as one might have
expected.

I must also acknowledge the help of a sabbatical leave
from the University of California, Los Angeles, and a grant
from the UCLA Research Committee. This last paid for, if
it could not suitably reward, the delightful diligence of my
research assistant, Elena Barcia. Finally, I must thank the
staff of the Yale Press. They have been everything an
author could wish his press to be.

R.A.L.

Los Angeles
1973

1 The Prose Problem and "The Books"

> Your damned nonsense can I stand twice or once, but
> sometimes always, my God, never.
>
> Svatislav Richter, to the second flute
> at Covent Garden

People have thought prose style many things—persuasion
or mere music, duty or pastime, ornament only, the man
himself. It has been left for Americans to think it a problem:
the National Problem, the Communications Problem. From
time to time we castigate our daily speech, but it is for
written utterance—for prose—that the true jeremiads are
reserved. These are hard to assess. Prophets of doom rarely
confess their prejudices. And for the American prose scene
the prejudices are many, and probably inevitable. As an
English commentator put it: "On subjects like America and
Prose one's mind cannot be made a blank."*

It is easy enough for the language teacher to deliver
himself of unarguable pronouncements, especially if these
reveal his calling to be crucial, unvalued, and underpaid.
Language provides the medium of conscious life, and those
professionally concerned with it ought often to point this
out. If language becomes truly unexpressive, we indeed
become a mob. With so much at stake, it should not surprise
us that the epithets for current American prose (and the
educational procedures which create it) are quick to damn.
Jacques Barzun's summary phrase, "Black Rot" may stand
as example. Yet the world has most often been arthritic
in its utterance. Whether our historical situation, our prose
problem, emerges as truly more severe than that of other
times or other countries, no one, with any hard evidence at
least, can at present judge. This problem, like so many of

---

* Geoffrey Moore, "American Prose Today," in *Essays on Language and
Usage*, eds. Leonard Dean and Kenneth Wilson, p. 351.

ours, seems unprecedented. No other country has ever
considered skill in prose composition essential to good
citizenship and has tried to teach this skill to a majority of
its citizens. The citizens of no other country have, so far,
undergone so heavy a verbal saturation by the media. The
scope and magnitude of our problems, their now-or-never
fundamentality, vastly increase the pressure on the means—
ultimately language—through which they are to be expressed and perhaps solved.

At the same time, our processes of education—and the
theories that underlie them—have been undergoing dislo-
cating stresses unequaled in the West since the Reforma-
tion. We do not know how much of what we loosely call
"communication" is written, how much oral, or what the
relationship between the two kinds is. We possess no
calculus of misunderstandings. "Failure of communication," our cant term for all occasions, often masks simple
vacancy of mind. A student writes on an examination
paper, "Abuses in the Church troubled Martin Luther
beyond belief." Does the fault lie with language or the
mind? We have no way of measuring the efficiency of our
schools in teaching good prose, for there are no agreed upon
standards of good prose and no standard of teaching
accomplishment to measure against.

Furthermore, the problem of prose—so large, so central—
introduces fundamental questions. What exactly *is* communication and how does it take place? What do we *mean* by
clarity? How may we separate clarity from special interest,
from attempts to persuade, or from correctness? Good prose
takes time. Is it always worth it? Does clear writing really
make for clear thinking? Are the criticisms of modern prose
directed at clarity or at elegance? Does elegance, or
eloquence, improve the communication of concepts? In an
increasingly oral technology, will we need written communication at all? Finally, if we are in a crisis of utterance, is it

civilization that is at stake, or only the joy and pleasure that literate people take in language?

The problem of prose, all this is to say, does not at present admit of scientific (quantitative) resolution, or even of scientific address. We do not know even the magnitude of the problem. As a Welfare Department spokesman once eloquently complained, "We're in a position where we're really not sure of what kind of a situation we're in." Humanists will hasten to add that such a problem should not—by its nature, cannot—profitably endure scientific scrutiny. You may agree, but it is hard to find the agreement reassuring. It leaves us in a shady universe of tentative hints and heuristic guesses. One would like to know at least the boundary conditions of the problem. All that we have now is a growing sense of muddled language, public and private. To this, those of us who teach prose will want to add an awareness of growing student ineptitude that it might not be too strong to call chilling. When I started teaching ten years ago, freshman writing was incorrect and misspelled. Now it is mindless.

To so vaguely defined a problem, one can scarcely speak of a coherent national response. But there has been that kind of activity which begins to define a problem, if not to solve it. It has come, obviously, through the schools and colleges. No one need anatomize again their performance in teaching students how to write. The schools' failures have been inevitable. Teaching grammar and composition takes a great deal of time, time no teacher in America is given. Because of this massive failure, the weight has fallen on a peculiar American institution, the college course in Freshman Composition. To this course, now ten weeks long or, for real depth, a full semester, come the tired, the poor, the huddled students yearning to be freed. Their training and experience vary from weak to nonexistent. The plan is to have them emerge at the end of the course writing prose as

limpid as a purling stream and as lean as a greyhound on a
diet. The miracle worker who presides over this classroom of
thirty to forty aspirants is often a graduate student. He may
be a first-year graduate student. He has not been trained to
teach prose composition. He may not write good prose
himself. He will teach two sections of such a course—in
hard times and places, three. He is a student himself, and
upon his performance as such depend his higher degree and
his escape from teaching Freshman Comp. Yet he is
exhorted to give his whole heart to this shortcut to oblivion.
But if he is observant, he will harbor little optimism about
what, even at best and at full time, he might accomplish in
one course.

Consider what he is trying to teach. The usual Freshman
Composition course takes as its subject something called
(old-fashion) Rhetoric or (new-fashion) Basic Communications Skills. New or old, it is basically the medieval trivium,
or first arts course, a progress of grammar, logic, and
rhetoric. The medieval student spent *all* his time on these
three *until he got his B.A.* Students now get ten weeks.
Invariably, these students know nothing of logic when they
begin, practically nothing of grammar, and often literally
do not know what rhetoric is. They do know that the course
is unimportant to their future academic careers. No professor, if they go into science, will expect them to write
comprehensible prose or penalize—and correct—them if
they do not. If they study social science, they will find the
lucid prose their eager teaching assistant urges upon them a
positive handicap. And even should they remain in the
English department, the chance of their being held to a
standard of good prose grows daily smaller.

There are more lurid colors for the vignette. Add that the
instructor may not know the rules of formal logic himself, or
the modern thinking that has almost transformed the
traditional subject. He will, more importantly, be aware
that in our time there are two "grammars," one traditional

and prescriptive, one usage-centered and "transforma-tional." Though they try to explain the same phenomena, the two stand poles apart. Each Freshman Composition class, depending on the text used and the instructor's knowledge and predilection, will offer a different mixture of the two. To so promising a pedagogical situation, add other influences. The Freshman Rhetoric course is formally required of, and thus resented by, all. In an age of few requirements, and those dwindling, it allegorizes cruel and unnatural punishment. Furthermore, the brightest students are often excused from it on the basis of their high-school performance. The rest feel themselves, not without reason, the Awkward Squad.

What is likely to be learned in such a course? In recent years many faculties, answering sensibly "Nothing at all," have abolished it. Nothing is offered in its place. Instead, a spontaneous game of "Let's Pretend" begins and the students' ineptitude is simply ignored. The problem that high schools gave up on and left to the colleges, the colleges now give up on and leave to the graduate schools, society, and God. Even if the class were to succeed, grounds for abolition might obtain. The amount of attention paid to changes in student writing ability over the undergraduate years is shockingly small. One excellent study by Albert R. Kitzhaber (*Themes, Theories, and Therapy: The Teaching of Writing in College*, 1963) would seem to constitute—though he had not the heart to press his conclusions so far—the best evidence yet for the uselessness of Freshman Composition. Kitzhaber studied Dartmouth College students—bright, carefully selected, and very energetically taught writing in the freshman year, for the most part by seasoned, degree-bearing, full-time faculty members. The students improved. But unless they majored in English, by their senior year they were back to square one. The students worked hard. The instructors worked even harder, graded ten to twenty thousand words a week of undergraduate writing, in detail, revisions submitted—the lot. Yet very little took, very little lasted. Even under optimal circumstances the course failed.

What has gone wrong? It would be comforting to think this failure only one of will and money. If Americans were willing to spend the truly vast sums needed for good schools, the schools themselves would solve the problem. If only the colleges had the money, in their hecatombs of English I sections they could solve it. The profession could see the problem, and bracing itself to its duty, do it. Yet even were this battalion of blessings to descend upon us, the problem would remain. Poverties of attitude, not only of funds, create it.

"It is the thought that really matters." This illusion runs deep in American society. It may account for the pervasive stylelessness of American life. It certainly explains the stylelessness of American prose. When American students sit down, having—sacred thing—"expressed themselves," and are required to revise what they have written, they feel—there is no other word for it—silly. Only a child would do this. What's the point in spending a lot of time prettying things up? The thought is what counts. Style is for your secretary, correctness something that is part of the typing. To be interested in it, especially for a man, is like being interested in furnishing his house—women's work. So, should a student, by guess or by God, actually learn something about prose style, he will find nobody in the society he speedily joins who knows or cares what good prose is, and nothing that encourages him to write well or rewards him if he does. The stupidest and most recalcitrant students of composition usually make the most sensible comment on the course: "Why should I care how I write when nobody else does?"

They are even more right than they know. They point to the joyous world beyond the confines of school and college, but few within the ivory tower know or care either. Professor Kitzhaber puts it fairly (pp. 119–20):

The only solution is a general conviction among students that good writing and good thinking are inseparable and that both are characteristic of a liberally educated adult. But students are not likely to develop this conviction as long as their other teachers in school and college so often reveal that they themselves lack it.

Criticizing prose style takes more than knowledge and experience. It takes time. The high-school teacher perhaps does not have the knowledge, and certainly not the time to develop the experience. As a result, students are sent to college who simply have never thought about prose style. And these students meet a professor who takes his delight in teaching and researching a *subject*, and that subject is seldom prose style. Thus the university, after the genuflection of Freshman Composition, ignores the problem as completely as does outside society. Good prose does not come from a one-time inoculation. It has to be sustained by the standards of a society, by that society's sense of style. It has to be encouraged, appreciated, rewarded. Its countervailing ugliness has to be mocked. None of this now happens in America. There may once have been enclaves in English departments that did these things. No more. Almost nowhere can an American experience good prose in his daily life or write it well. He is never encouraged to pay attention to language.

It is precisely this act of attention which American students find so awkward, so artificial, in prose-style instruction. If you ask an American student to read a prose passage aloud, he sits paralyzed with fright. It is not simply that he has never in his life read one aloud, though this is often true. It is that he must pay attention to words in a new way, and he finds this acutely uncomfortable. Americans use their language, spoken as well as written, in a chronic absence of mind. To open ears and eyes to language is as painful as to drive down a city street and actually look at it. The ugliness, attended to, stripped of familiarity, appalls.

The attitude toward prose, then, is part of a larger attitude toward environment, especially man-made environment. In both, the American experience teaches and enforces the same response. Blindness. The result, as the following pages demonstrate, is writing not so much incorrect or unclear—though it is usually both—as simply unseeing.

Our society, then, offers no positive reinforcement (as the psychologists call it) to good prose, no negative to bad. Still worse, it offers positive reinforcement to the bad, negative to the good. The media, as one would expect, reflect and exacerbate the American attitude toward language. Words are to use. Advertising, in supplying plastic soul to the media, literally *uses up* words for profit. It parodies divinity in turning the word into matter, into goods. Every day of his life, an American encounters the word primarily in someone's effort to sell him something. He must train himself to look through the word to the trap beneath. Enjoy the language and they've got you. Karl Shapiro called advertising the poetry of the poor. It is the poetry of us all—a poetry that travesties poetry, where the words never exist for themselves, where their dignity, shape, form is never respected, where they are perpetually for sale. Advertising is America's real composition class, its real training in prose style. Faced with advertising, the dedicated teacher of prose composition is like the saintly fireman in the cliché, charging hell with a bucket of ice water.

It is instructive to compare the English with the American tradition of thinking about prose style. The English tradition has been a strongly normative one, but unstated. Good prose, in a common phrase, is like good manners. Everyone may be expected to recognize it and use it without fuss. The rich literary tradition underlying any kind of sensitivity to prose style is likewise assumed. Thus, if you pick up one of the standard discussions of prose written by an Englishman (see Read, Murry, Sutherland, and Lucas in my bibliographical note), you find that it draws contin-

ually on—and supposes familiarity with—the whole range
of English literature, and often Continental texts as well.
Only with such a grounding can a prose style in English
really be understood, be experienced.

Prose may be a "problem" for us as it has never been for
the English, precisely because we lack both the literary and
the social norms that give it meaning. We can assume
neither a norm of gentility nor a literary tradition. Teachers
of prose in America are often at a loss when asked to
recommend studies of style. Such studies almost invariably
talk about it in terms of texts the student has never heard of.
One English theorist recommends, as a useful means for
testing conciseness in English prose, quick translation into
Latin or Greek. Americans, students or not, live in another
world. They are trying to learn something about prose style
without the whole context that has rendered prose style
comprehensible and has given it meaning. They are trying
to learn in a vacuum. And we may, of course, add as a
footnote to the contemporary scene, the much-heralded
demise of the book. Americans used to read only current
fiction. Now they read nothing at all. For written utterance,
they have as context only journalism. How accurate such
prophecies of doom really are, I suppose few would want to
say. But the teacher of composition, at whatever level, will
speedily be reminded that he is trying to teach prose to
people who, at least voluntarily, seldom read *anything*.

A comment by an English translator about American
translations points shrewdly to our central difficulty:

In their own tongue Americans fear no obscurity, no imprecision.
When it comes to rendering a foreign page into American English
they are hampered, however, by a puritan distrust for words.
Normal Americans have a very small vocabulary. They feel
towards words as they feel towards the parts of a car: let them
function; no more is asked of them. [Alan Pryce Jones, "Translations and the Americans," *Times Literary Supplement*, Sept. 25,
1970.]

"They feel towards words as they feel towards the parts of a car." This attitude underlies the prose problem in America. We *use* words but we don't really *like* them. Such an attitude is implicit not only in courses in composition but in the society as a whole. The assumption is Jeffersonian. The best prose style is the one that styles the least. In the best of all possible worlds, there would not be any words at all to mislead, only concepts. Surely this discomfort with words galvanizes our delight in computers, mechanical people who speak a language masticated into binary bits. In a throwaway culture, words, like everything else, are to be got rid of. If, as I argue here, prose style begins in pleasure and not in clarity, the throwaway assumption defeats us before we begin.

American pragmatism insists that words are for use, not enjoyment; American puritanism insists that expression is a duty, not a pleasure. We dislike learning foreign languages because such learning requires taking pleasure in words for themselves. Let all the world learn one language (English, of course, and our brand of English) so that we can do away with verbal misunderstandings and get down to brass tacks. We learn to speedread our own language for the same reason. Such an attitude becomes a self-fulfilling prophecy. Prose written without joy can only be read in the same spirit. Given the average quality of American prose, speedreading it out of existence is probably the best thing. So we come to hate the word, and use it still more ineffectively. "No profit goes where is no pleasure ta'en."

Just as our scientific attempts to "conquer" nature end by destroying and dehumanizing it, our efforts to Do our Duty as Effective Communicators end up holding language at arm's length. We pare away all sense of verbal play, of self-satisfying joy in language, and then wonder why American students have a motivation problem and don't want to write. A literate, reading culture imbibes its joy in language naturally, through its literary experiences. Poetry

is, after all, language in a state of play. No readers we,
denied this source of joy, we then devise a pedagogy that
denies every other source as well. We want to degrade all
verbal pleasure into utility, just as we degrade all human
motive into the cash nexus. And the utilitarian premise,
simplified as it is, yet proves false. Good prose no more
makes a man thrive in the world than does higher
education as a whole. Look at the rich and the famous.
John Jay Chapman said all this long ago:

Now, the truth is that the higher education does not advance a
man's personal interests except under special circumstances.
What it gives a man is the power of expression; but the ability to
express himself has kept many a man poor. [*Learning and Other
Essays* (1910), p. 33]

Articulate speech can get you in trouble. Conversely, if you
really are great with child to speak, you can get the message
across, as did Richter to the second flute at Covent Garden,
without speaking the language at all. So instruction in
composition builds on a single premise—clarity—and that
premise is false.

   The simplifications of Freshman Composition are, then,
the simplifications of American life. America has faced the
prose problem with a characteristically confident attitude,
intensely practical on the one hand and high-mindedly
moralistic on the other. As a practical matter, we need as
much prose style as will get the world's business done
expeditiously—a philosophy of denotative clarity—and are
willing to pay for only this much and no more. On the other
hand, civilization does depend on the state of our native
language, and so our approach to the problem of prose style
must be unremittingly moral. A typically American commandment is thus precipitated out: Thou shalt be as clear
as necessary in order that the world's business be done
efficiently and civilization thereby preserved. A broad
justification, then, for a narrow theory of prose style. Upon

this disjunctive and sometimes contradictory yoking of use
and morality has been built the prose pedagogy of America.

We concentrate on utility at the expense of *joie de vivre*.
And we then wonder, as De Tocqueville prophesied we
would, why life has lost its savor. We rediscover, in fact, the
utilitarian value of pleasure. We have begun to do this in
American life, perhaps, but not in teaching prose style.
There, a pompous moralism still prevails:

> So delicate are the adjustments of thought and language, so many
> and diverse the differences in the unknown and unnumbered
> persons we would reach, so great the chances of failure and so
> slender the assurance of success, that we need a more rigorous
> devotion, a stricter purpose: to speak and write not merely so as to
> be understandable,—but so as to be *unmistakable*. Nothing less
> stern will pull our slackness up to exactitude and make our
> slouching erect and vertebrate. [H. Robinson Shipherd, *The Fine
> Art of Writing*, pp. 13–14]

Surely we ought to move in the opposite direction from such
moral earnestness, stressing not words as duty but words as
play. Our efforts to cope with the National Prose Problem
might more avail, be finally more utilitarian, if they were
willing to embrace a purpose richer and more humane than
joyless—and useless—utility. Our national efforts may lack
not so much money as imagination. "Speech in its essence,"
Kenneth Burke tells us, "is not neutral" (*Permanence and
Change*, p. 176); it is full of feeling, attitude, emotion. Drain
this out in the name of useful unmistakability and you end
up with composition-class prose, a dismal grayness which,
like so much of American life, seems significant only of its
own insignificance. And the spirit of play, the spontaneous
joy in words, banished from the front door, will only, as we
shall later see, sneak in through the back.

The fundamental problems of prose in America, then, are
social as well as pedagogical. How might the study of style
best address them? Such study has always been cursed by

two perplexities. A course in writing has no immediate context—it is not writing *for* anything—and it has no *subject.* What do you write *about?* Until prose style concerns everyone, and not just English departments, the first question can find only incomplete answers. Students will remain flaccid and unmotivated until some connection is made between writing and the motives their culture really honors. Perhaps the best way to insure "A" papers would be to pay a cash reward. Until we attain that golden sequel, surely what is called for is a theory of prose composition which stresses its pleasures as well as its duties, and supplies some kind of context for these pleasures.

To answer this second question—What do you write about?—generations of impecunious pedagogues have racked their brains. Look-in-your-heart-and-write Sincerity ("My Most Exciting Day at The Beach," "What God Really Means to Me"), Current Events ("Rotten Senator X," "The Slanted Prose of Magazine Y," "The Heart-rending Pickle of Minority Z"), Still Life ("A Rhododendron in the Rain")—the search for novelty has been desperate. Surely the question permits a simpler answer.

There is only one inevitable *subject* for a course in writing, writing itself—style. Paul Roberts has thought the great contribution of linguistics to writing instruction to be that linguistics itself becomes the subject ("The Relation of Linguistics to the Teaching of English," *College English,* October 1960). A sampling of the crabgrass prose of linguists scarcely gets our hopes up. Worse, the scientific set of linguistics moves the student in precisely the wrong direction. He should be looking *at* the stylistic surface; instead, he is continually invited to look through it to a deep structure beneath. He is encouraged, again, to attend not to style but to something beyond it. Any writing course in America today should aim at an acute self-consciousness about style. For this purpose, style itself must be the object of contemplation. Writing courses usually stress, not style, but rhetoric's other two traditional parts, finding arguments and arranging them. Yet both, implicit in a study of style, emerge naturally only from a concentration on it. If a student really cannot think logically to begin with, he needs another course. Writing prose will be beyond him. Composition should not be asked to do too much. Its natural subject is style.

Composition texts have not seen it this way. They stand foursquare on the trivium. In fact, they try to include everything. General Acceptability lies heavy upon them. The publishers, to ensure big sales, have them certified ninny-proof by boards of special advisers. Perhaps this is why most of them bore us so. They have a special tone, the tone you use to a child old enough to understand but who doesn't, to a foreigner looking for the bathroom who you're not sure really understands the language. Big, heavy, textbooky, with endpaper polychrome charts, they make the heart sink just to look at them. They have been variously traduced as fast-buck work, but this gives a false impression. They seem nothing if not laborious. They aim to take in a typical freshman, gawky and clueless, process him cover to cover, and turn out a conflation of Walter Pater and George Orwell. No questions have been spared, no exhortations finessed, no error uncatalogued or unabbreviated into a superefficient squirrel chatter of *uncs, orgs, parals,* and *logs.* No, it is not earnestness that composition texts lack. It is joy. Their earnestness lies upon the spirit like wet cardboard. The moral imperative above all characterizes these texts, a bizarre class of endeavor which, as I made my way through them, spontaneously christened themselves "The Books."

Good prose, The Books tell us, is a duty. Their conception of prose is utilitarian and moral. If language is the means of conscious life, then Good Prose, like Cleanliness, must stand next to Godliness. This perpetual moralizing about language haunts all modern writing about style. So

Aldous Huxley, that new-model sunday school teacher and papier-mâché sage on "Words and their Meanings":

When Gotama insisted on Right Speech, when Jesus stressed the significance of every idle word, they were not lecturing on the theory of semiosis; they were inculcating the practice of the highest virtues. Words and the meanings of words are not matters, merely for the academic amusement of linguists and logicians, or for the aesthetic delight of poets; they are matters of the profoundest ethical significance to every human being.

Perhaps it was his American audience (a Los Angeles audience, as you can tell—Buddha is addressed by his familiar name) that prompted Huxley to such sobriety. Because Americans do not think words important at all, writers about words must call them vital. Thus in The Books, in most writing about style, the imperative mood prevails. Here is a list of exhortative chapter headings from one of The Books:

> Do not take yourself too seriously
> Consider your readers
> Make your writing talk
> Be a good mechanic
> Sharpen your thesis
> Believe in your thesis
> Build your essay in three parts

What can you say? What can you ever say to Polonius? A student, if he is on scholarship or has an ambitious mother, may actually try to earn all these merit badges. But if he has any spirit, he'll murmur a well-chosen four-letter word and go out and get stoned. Or if he is exceptionally thoughtful, he may explore the contradictions embedded in these commandments.

"What is 'too seriously'"? "Why *three* parts?" "How can I believe in a thesis obviously hoked up for English 1?" "Write from a suitable design"? You might as well say "Be Intelligent." In fact that's what all The Books' mottoes come down to, isn't it? Why not just pass out wall plaques reading "Don't Screw It Up Again!"

Students of style are bombarded with self-canceling clichés. Here's a quintessence taken from The Books published in the last hundred years.

> Be Plain; Avoid "fine writing"
> Avoid Bluntness; Articulate your sentences gracefully
> Make your writing spontaneous
> Revise!
> Be yourself
> Imitate the masters
> Write from your own experience
> Read widely ("A man will turn over half a library to make one book," Samuel Johnson is repeatedly quoted as saying)
> Make an Outline
> Don't over-outline
> Be serious without being stuffy
> Study spoken speech
> Writing and Speaking are different things
> What the prose writer needs is a temperament nicely balanced between the sprightly and the phlegmatic, a lively mind and a deliberate judgment. His ideas will flow easily, but not too impetuously.

And, on a larger scale, Dickens and Buffon advise that writing talent is an infinite capacity for taking pains. Edward S. Martin disagrees: "I don't think writing can be taught much beyond the rudiments. The rest of it seems to come from the teacher who runs the singing classes for the birds." All this advice, totaled up, yields "Nothing succeeds like success." "Success," of course, is never specifically defined. Sir Herbert Read, in *English Prose Style* (p. xii), writes:

But is there an abstract entity, an absolute or "pure" style, to which all styles approximate, or against which all styles are judged? I think there probably is, but it follows from my definition of prose that such a style can never be defined.

This difficulty doesn't bother Sir Herbert as much as it ought to. For it exposes what we might call the Fallacy of Normative Prose. All prose style cherishes a single goal and that goal is to disappear. The aim is the same for all: clarity, denotation, conceptual fidelity. The imperative of imperatives in The Books is "Be clear." The best style is the never-noticed. Ideally, prose style should, like the state under Marxism, wither away, leaving the plain facts shining unto themselves.

One of the difficulties Freshman Composition has faced, then, though The Books take no notice of it, is trying to teach the invisible, to discuss something that, ideally, isn't there at all. In a real and literal sense, The Books have argued their subject out of existence. They do not teach style, they abolish it. And it is around this fascinating vacuum that the American fetish for correctness, the agony over those droll Victorian antimacassars "usage" and "abusage," so resolutely assembles.

Anyone who dips into The Books soon sees that their advice runs to a dreary sameness. Yet successful prose styles vary as widely as the earth. A hundred different styles cannot be accurately described by a single set of apothegms, eulogistic or dyslogistic. That the transparent prose norm, that reified nonentity Expository Prose, leaves out all prose fiction and nine-tenths of nonfictional prose ought at least to have *troubled* someone. People seldom write simply to be clear. They have designs on their fellow men. Pure prose is as rare as pure virtue, and for the same reasons. The classical discussions of style concern themselves less with clarity than with more common human purposes, with advantage and pleasure. But The Books, written for a man and world yet unfallen, depict a ludicrous process like this: "I have an idea. I want to present this as a gift to my fellow man. I fix this thought clearly in mind. I follow the rules. Out comes a prose that gift-wraps thought in transparent paper." If this sounds like a travesty, it's because it is one. Yet it dominates prose instruction in America. Prose composition masquerades as a one-step operation that aims to communicate concepts.

The Books seldom tantalize themselves with large hopes, but let us imagine their dream world come true. A world neither too short nor too long, neither formal nor familiar, impersonal nor idiosyncratic, neither too spontaneous nor too carefully revised. A bore. Such a world would be as tedious as the heavenly paradise on which it is so embarrassingly modeled. Talleyrand, an expert at living in the fallen world, thought language was invented so that man could *conceal* what he really thinks. This Kierkegaard improved to "so that he can hide the fact that he doesn't think at all." Both come closer to the truth than The Books' simplistic paradigm.

The American blindness to style is intensified by such a paradigm. Once again, down with words and up with ideas. The Books march off dutifully to precisely the wrong battle. The pedagogy of style in America ought to *contradict* this fixation, not reinforce it. Such a strategy will be simplistic, but in the opposite direction. The prevailing wind bloweth toward meaning, toward concept on the one hand and morality on the other; let us blow toward style, verbal pattern. Such a procedure involves an exaggeration, but one more faithful to the real nature of prose. The Books, when they teach clarity as be-all and end-all, teach an extravagant simplification, a simplification that students often sense though seldom articulate.

I propose an alternative goal: not clarity, but a self-conscious pleasure in words. Such self-consciousness is the only stylistic attitude likely to last beyond the classroom. The only prose didacticism likely to work in America is auto-didacticism, and the only possible basis for such teaching is an acute awareness of stylistic surface. Everything in a composition course should be directed toward such an aim. Not clarity but attention must come first. Only such a therapy will compensate for the literary tradition that even literate Americans do not possess. Only such an emphasis will aerate the vacuum of stylelessness into which prose-style teaching evaporates, will provide the reinforcement that society fails to offer. Only such self-consciousness will equip Americans to cope with the verbiage that surrounds them, to banquet off the nonsense.

What we have now is a tedious, repetitive, unoriginal body of dogma—clarity, sincerity, plainness, duty—tarted up every week in a new, disposable paperback dress. The dogma of clarity, as we shall see, is based on a false theory of knowledge; its scorn of ornament, on a misleading taxonomy of style; the frequent exhortations to sincerity, on a naïve theory of the self; and the unctuous moralizing, on a Boy Scout didacticism. Instruction in style ought to concentrate on what can be taught. Goethe, in his conversations with Eckermann, is reputed to have said that "if any man would write in a noble style let him first possess a noble soul." Wonderful, but not much help. It may be, though some wise men have denied it, that virtue can be taught, but it seems unlikely that it can be taught in Freshman Composition. Nor sincerity. Nor spontaneity. Nor true grit. What can be taught is words. And they must be taught in the full matrix of human utterance, written and spoken, accompanied by a theory of style equally broad. A student bright enough to be taught style needs a context for it beyond didactic precept, an intelligible and sound context. Style cannot be taught only by lists of self-contradicting proverbs, strings of do's and don'ts. Students so instructed are not being taught; they are being housebroken.

I recommend, in what follows, a particular strategy for a particular time and place. Prose style cannot be taught, as it has been, in—and as—a vacuum. It will simply end up, as has been happening with increasing frequency (vacuums being hard to teach), not being taught at all. It cannot be taught as a duty, for you cannot teach as duty what society does not feel a duty. Style must be taught for and as what it is—a pleasure, a grace, a joy, a delight. Pleasure will not, it is true, teach the dumb to speak, the stupid to write, or the bad to practice goodness. But neither will anything else.

2 The Uses of Obscurity

Dic, aliquem sodes hic, Quintiliane, colorem. haeremus
[Quick, Quintilian, an excuse, for Heaven's sake. I'm stuck.]
Juvenal 6. 280–81

"D'abord la clarté" Anatole France exhorts us, "puis encore la clarté, et enfin la clarté"—clarity first, last, and always. No one has ever disagreed. "Prose," John Middleton Murry tells us in *The Problem of Style* (p. 52), "is the language of exact thinking; it was made for the purpose; and I suppose that a proposition in Euclid is an elementary example of good style, though in an absolutely noncreative kind." The Books build upon clarity as upon a rock. Good prose stands like a well-washed window giving onto the Kingdom of Thought. "It is good prose when it allows the writer's meaning to come through with the least possible loss of significance and nuance, as a landscape is seen through a clear window" (Sutherland, *On English Prose*, p. 77). In such a race, either Swift or Dryden usually finishes first, with lesser seventeenth- and eighteenth-century stylists down the field. Before then, since then, and in America of course always, it has been downhill. Such a style, as this theorist continues, "was too good to last."

Scholars have the right, of course, to issue prescriptive definitions of anything at all, and certainly of good prose. But as a description of what prose has actually been like and done, this definition ought to strike us as hopelessly inadequate—preposterous, in fact. It describes with any accuracy the prose of only a very few writers, and does not really, as we shall see, even describe them. To use Swift as norm or sanction for an everlasting "Be clear" simply leaves most prose out of contention. ("The continued vitality of Swift's style is a great consolation to the theorists," Sir Herbert Read reassures us.)

People, even literary people, seldom content themselves with being clear. They invent jargons, argot, odd ways of being clear. They impose nefarious designs upon their neighbors. They repeat things for the pleasure of repetition. They usually swim in a muddy ineptitude, and even when they succeed in being clear it is often only to seem clever. You would think, from the unexamined god-term Clarity has become, that students of prose had never heard of nonreferential language—emotional, phatic, symbolic, purely social. A wholly denotative prose is found as seldom as a purely denotative poetry. People are just not that way. "Be clear!" The moral version, "Be good!" offers as much help. No one would *disagree*. But such moral coordinates do not describe prose in a fallen world. Clarity stands indeed as a laudable aim. If we are willing to define it broadly enough, it may stand for all laudable aims. But narrow or broad, it needs examination.

The university, you might think, would be the place, if any, to find clarity most in demand, most sought-after and applauded. We might, then, apply the clarity touchstone to some typical academic prose. Consider these three examples, selected at reasonable random. (I did select for a student-professor-administrator cross-section.)

A letter from an undergraduate to the student newspaper:

The fall quarter is coming to an end. Although this is not surprising in itself, the "Bell Syndrome" is. Students on this campus must become cognizance [*sic*] of the fact that those students that succumb to the "Bell Syndrome" has facilitated others to escape. Those students which pass a course satisfactorily should be aware that individual achievement alone did not accomplish this. In part, it was accomplished at the expense of other students to the "Bell Syndrome."

Moreover, it should be obvious that one way to increase admissions to the University without necessarily increasing the total population of the University is to enforce the bell shape distribution of grades. This will ultimately take its toll of college students.

The goals of education has become obfuscated at the high school level and this is manifested as high school "drop outs." Likewise at the college level, students that succumb to the "Bell Syndrome" are college "put outs."

The inoculation against the "Bell Syndrome" will necessitate an all out effort on the part of all students to ensure no one falls victim of it.

Tolerance of the "Bell Syndrome" only perpetuate the existing system. Students that confess to greater involvement in the community-at-large are only deluding themselves because of their continued tolerance of the "Bell Syndrome."

Has it not occurred to students that some of the constituents of the community may comprise victims of the "Bell Syndrome" which facilitate a greater chasm in relationship than already exist.

If students cannot relate to other students, how can they relate to the community. Students must not allow the umbra of the "Bell Syndrome" to abort the self-determination of fellow students.

Armed with clarity, we can obviously have a romp in this *hortus deliciarum* of adolescent indignation. The author, we might begin by suggesting, should not be allowed to die a natural death. A junior, presumably in good standing in—needless to say—the Sociology department, he cannot yet hold subject and verb in agreement ("Tolerance . . . only perpetuate," "the goals . . . has become," "students . . . has facilitated"), does not know noun from adjective ("cognizance" for "cognizant"), has trouble locating the relative pronoun used for people ("those students that," "those students which"), falls victim to the dangling prepositional phrase ("to the Bell Syndrome"), has a weakness for the half-understood word, big or unusual ("obfuscated," "umbra," "comprise," "abort"), and loves to coin terms in the best tradition of social science ("put outs," "Bell Syndrome"). He puts together in fresh combinations words he has often heard but never understood. How, for example, do you facilitate a chasm? If someone's umbra aborts your self-determination, do you sue? He seems to think, not simply with clichés, but wholly in predigested phrases: the idiotic "this is not surprising in itself" in the second line, for example, or "constituents of the community" comprising "victims."

What does such prose reveal? Is clarity the problem? Perhaps because the argument is familiar, I can, except for the penultimate paragraph, follow it with a little work. If grades are assigned on a curve, some will rise because others fall. The student has observed that, though some classes may perform so as to fit the curve naturally, others do not. The student has obviously not said *exactly* what he means— merciful heaven—but he has, all he would doubtless profess to want, "communicated." Why, then, is our response to the letter so prompt? That is, not only a "My God, what prose!" but as Stephen Leacock put it, "Willie is no good. We'll sell him."

First, I suppose, comes skirling, scornful laughter at his elementary mistakes of grammar. This, a social judgment, probably dominates any literate reader's response to the letter. But still more than its mistaken grammar, its ugliness stands out. It is not simply that the writer has no feeling for the shape or rhythm of his sentences. (Paragraph four is a good example of this shapelessness.) They are full of unintended sound patterns, "rel*ate*," "necessit*ate*," "facili*tate*"; "*c*onstituents of the *c*ommunity may *c*omprise." The writer feels indignant and indignation demands eloquence. Instead, we see him floundering, dramatizing helpless irritation. The letter is unintentionally expressive. The Books would call the problem clarity, but that doesn't describe it. His prose, just barely an adequate vehicle for his thesis, communicates a great deal besides, and this extra communication undermines the thesis.

In the terms of classical rhetoric, the writer has established a disastrous ethos, or public dramatization of character—what we call image. This ruins his case. The bell syndrome can't be all bad if it threatens a donkey like him. The student has not failed to communicate; he has communicated too well. "Be clear," in this case, would mean eliminating the unintentional revelation of ignorance and folly. The clarity argument ignores the unfailing expressivity of words. The real error comes in the presentation of the writer's self. And, of course, there is nothing—at least for the present, and in his case probably for the future—that the writer can do about his self. Thus when The Books tell him, "Be clear," they are saying, with the Good Book, with the Gospels, "Be born again." The futility of such advice ought to be more apparent than it is. Such prose as this testifies to problems of training and raw intelligence far beyond any power of prose style to cure.

Talking, then, about how the writer communicates a concept leads precisely in the wrong direction here. Dramatization of character demands center stage. If we moralize about what a violation of the sacred-scientific-duty-to-express-concepts-clearly has been committed, we ignore the point and hence fail to help the student—if that is possible. The prophecy of doom will be greeted by the student at all events with an echoing scorn ("Who knows the difference? Who cares?"), which the following selections from his academic superiors do little to dispel.

Consider this memo from a professor.

The Task Force is also concerned that it provide the basis for the faculty of this campus to govern itself, rather than being governed by others less understanding of the nature of the University. Consequently, we are asking you to specify the methods you use to evaluate the effectiveness of your instruction. Likewise, we are seeking your views on the function of evaluation and your suggestions for the implementation of evaluation of instruction on a campus-wide basis. This information will greatly contribute to our recommendations regarding the best possible methods for evaluation of instruction which will at the same time be most acceptable to the greatest number of faculty possible, keeping in mind that diverse forms of evaluation will probably be called for in the face of the diverse functions and characteristics of this institution.

All information will be treated confidentially unless we have your specific permission to reference any of your statements.

This prose is clear enough. The problem is speed. It takes a long time to wade through the bureaucratese. A more accomplished stylist, or someone more impatient to be understood, might have said: "If we don't police the quality of instruction ourselves, someone else will. How do you tell whether you are doing a good job? May we quote you? Your method may be helpful in the tricky job of policing a colleague's teaching." But such a translation into plain English would lose much of what the passage really says. In the student's letter, the range of expressivity outside the boundary of plainness was not intended. No one deliberately proclaims himself an ass. Here, whether the professor intended such a proclamation or not seems unclear. Certainly no one could invent his tin ears deliberately.

Listen to the *sound* of "Likewise, we are seeking your views on the func*tion* of evalua*tion* and your sugges*tions* for the implementa*tion* of evalua*tion* of instruc*tion* on a campus-wide basis." This jangle of "shuns," of like word-endings (in classical rhetorical theory it bore—when intentional—the impressive name of *homoioteleuton*), betrays a man for whom prose has no sound. And, since he never re-creates the sound of prose by reading it aloud, his sentences have no shape or rhythm. Such writers often have recourse to endless strings of prepositional phrases that creep like a wounded snake across the page. Try circling the prepositions in the passage. Sentences, for a stylist like this, are likely to be long, labyrinthine, without natural emphasis— so the sentence beginning "This information," which winds its slow length through the second half of the first paragraph. This ineptitude, probably neither a failure to "have something to say" nor "to say it clearly," springs from a deafness to the *sound* of words and a resulting blindness to sentence *shape*. Clarity, in the semantic sense, intelligible utterance of concept, does not suffer here. If by clarity we mean euphony, rhythm, syntactical balance, shape, and grace, then we have expanded *clarity* to be synonymous with style.

But a dimension of expressivity inheres in the memo which, though undeclared to the reader, may subconsciously have been intended by the writer. The writer, chairman of a task force, is an aspiring academic bureaucrat. He must sound important, and make his Task Force sound more so. The plain prose paraphrase I have supplied fails both these purposes. If I say "Different kinds of teaching are to be judged differently," I am not saying clearly what the professor phrases as "keeping in mind that diverse forms of evaluation will probably be called for in the face of the diverse functions and characteristics of this institution." To the licensed bureaucrat, the plain version seems automatically suspicious. It sounds flip. The writer may not be taking his problem, and above all himself, with sufficient seriousness. Read a little more deeply. Evaluation of teaching is the touchiest subject on campus to the faculty right now. *Anything* you say is going to offend someone. A windy, free-floating verbosity presents itself as the best tactic. "Be clear" is disastrous advice.

Just put yourself in the writer's place. He knows, as does any teacher, that you judge the immediate effect of your instruction by contact with your class. You read their faces, worry about the pace of your lectures, revise them, change the pace in a recitation section, see how the papers and exams go, talk to students. Any teacher involved with his job *knows* how his teaching is going. You can tell that he knows—and how it went—just by looking at his posture after a class. The writer may know this. But he also knows that many of his colleagues are, in the sense of the word *teacher* that this sketch implies, not teachers at all. They do not read their students' papers or tests, see as little of them as possible, do not prepare much less revise their lectures, neither know nor care how well they teach. The writer of the memo knows, as do the receivers of it, that the sudden interest in undergraduate teaching is itself to the last degree hypocritical, and that no one actually expects a colleague to interrupt his research (or his lassitude) and dive into teaching. University professors are, however, expected to come up with a bureaucratic gesture ("a fresh evaluation of their teaching") in reply to the Task Force's bureaucratic gesture. That way, everybody is covered. If the student body president complains about poor teaching, he can be "shun-"ted off with evaluations, recommendations, implementations, and new functions for new institutions. These will be welcome to the student body president, of course, because he himself plays apprentice bureaucrat.

The memo, then, given the writer's purpose, succeeds very well. Fuurthermore, to those who know how to read it, it must seem as clear as day. To complain that the writer uses *reference* as a verb, that he has tin ears, that a sentence for him is a shopping bag he stuffs words into, that he comes across as a pompous humbug—all this misses the point. If he wrote the kind of prose The Books recommend, he would lose his job. Prose style does not work in a vacuum, except in Freshman Composition. It works in a context. The context makes it what it is. If you don't consider context, and often in some detail, you will not understand the prose style. A schoolmarmly "Tut, tut" is no substitute for understanding.

If the first passage dramatizes ineptitude, and the second a mixture of ineptitude and intended opacity, the following one seems wholly in the range of intention, a fully self-conscious document of style.

Letter from a chief administrative officer to his faculty:

In the face of both the severity and continuing character of the budgetary stringencies which we thus face, we have concluded

that we must undertake an immediate and thorough program-
matic review and re-ordering of academic priorities—a review
that would have been required in any event, although, perhaps,
on a less intensive time scale. We are convinced that it is no
longer possible to temporize and that action must soon be taken to
assure that those elements of our program which are essential to
the maintenance of a quality institution are protected and
nurtured through consolidation, reduction, and elimination of
those other elements which are found upon examination to be
inessential or which can be rendered more economical or efficient
through organizational or other changes. This process, to be
effective, must of course go beyond this Campus to the program of
the University as a whole. Indeed, it is increasingly clear that we
must press for a prompt reassessment of the University's Growth
Plan in the light of reduced fiscal expectations and seek an
appropriate reordering of priorities.

Accordingly, discussions have been initiated with leaders of the
Senate, and procedures are being established for the prompt
development and coordinated review of proposals for such
changes.

It is anticipated that the formal process will begin within a
month, dealing with these aspects of the academic program which
at the outset appear to promise most immediate and substantial
returns with minimal qualitative loss. It is intended, however, that
the process be extended beyond its initial scope through a
continuing campus-wide effort at re-evaluation and self-examina-
tion. At first these efforts must naturally reflect our reduced
budgetary expectations; however, the process is intended to
provide an effective means for future planning in anticipation of
an eventual return to more nearly adequate levels of support.
Indeed, we want, to the extent possible under current time
constraints, to identify desirable long-range goals and work back
to realistic intermediate positions which will lead to their
realization.

Taken in the abstract, in a stylistic universe of grace and
elegance, such utterance makes a lover of prose long to slide
into a warm bath and open a vein. For it is vintage
bureaucratese. Yet, in context, it becomes both comprehen-

sible and, in today's world of hokum, inevitable. The
university this president directs had just learned of massive
budget cuts—cuts, furthermore, coming for a second succes-
sive year after several lean years. Worse still, the cuts
included, again for the second year, no raise for the
faculty—not even a cost-of-living increase. The faculty,
then, the recipients of the letter, were both annoyed and
demoralized. What he had to say to them, had he drafted it
for a (slightly liberated) Freshman Composition course,
would have read like this:

Look, guys. The campus is broke this year. We've used up our
surplus. With the money we've got we can't do everything. We've
got to decide what things we can do well, do them, and stop doing
a good many others. We have to plan for the kind of future
limited budgets can create.

But how ham-handed, given the bureaucratic situation,
such a mode of address would be. If you are telling a man
he is going to take a cut in salary, that hard times are here
again, you had better be long-winded, dismal, above all
formal. That shows (1) that you *see* the gravity of the
situation, (2) that you *feel* the gravity of the situation as he
does, (3) that you are the kind of sober and reliable fellow
who can *deal with* the situation.

Consider another aspect. What the message really says is
that some people are going to be fired ("terminated"), some
departments shut down ("phased out"), some administrative kingdoms toppled ("programmatically reviewed"). The
whole passage, with this in mind, becomes an elaborate
exercise in euphemism. Some, in the event, were actually
fooled. But those in danger got the message loud and clear
and raised vociferous objections. The prose must be seen as
an attempt to forestall such objections, to pretend less stands
at stake, above all to project a certain attitude toward what
is at stake. The plain-prose mentality would have said to
the Speech department, "Look, something's got to go.

Much better you than Physics or History." But that is precisely the personality, the ethos, the writer did not want to project. Such utterance would betray both resolution and the settled attitude of a man with personal convictions. As written, we have the fair, aloof, indeed Olympian yet concerned, judgment of a disinterested technocrat. With malice toward none and compassion for all, he grasps the helm and faces the troubled waters ahead. If you find yourself, in the judgement of such a man, "found to be inessential" or "rendered more economical or efficient through organizational or other changes," how can you resent it? Resent *ineluctable economic process?*

We must consider, too, the writer's position. What he has to say is simple to the point of schoolboyishness: "We're broke. We've got to save some money. How to do it?" To which the underpaid professor mumbles, "We need you at $50,000 a year, to tell us this?" A group of students on whom I tried out the reductive paraphrase responded immediately, "He couldn't say that. Sure, it would be clearer, but it wouldn't sound like a college president." Of course not; and so a special language, like unto a royal proclamation, must be devised. Remote, impersonal ("It is intended that" not "I am going to"), euphemistic ("reduced budgetary expectations"), decisive yet not hasty ("We are convinced that it is no longer possible to temporize and that action must soon be taken to assure," rather than "We've got to do something"), the prose style does not seek to be clear but to *define a situation* and a personal role within that situation. In these terms it makes great sense.

And, for those who speak the language, those for whom prose is a problem, an opportunity perhaps, but hardly a pleasure, he spoke crystals of clarity. Watch academic bureaucrats being massaged by such prose. They smile slightly, settle a bit into the awkward lecture-room chairs, the musculature relaxes. They feel at home. The president is being clear. And if he does not Build His Essay in Three

Parts or Sharpen His Thesis, no one notices. He has Believed His Thesis and Considered His Readers and all is light.

Clarity (as central normative standard for "good prose") does more harm than good. For clarity is not any single verbal configuration but a relationship between writer and reader. There are all kinds of clarities. The kind The Books build upon, though we may applaud it in an aesthetic vacuum, seldom lives in the world of events, advantage, and pleasure, in the world where most prose lives, moves, has its being. When you say that a prose is clear, you are rewarding success, but the success may be of many kinds, the rewarding for many reasons. Thus the injunction "Be clear!" really amounts to "Succeed!", "Write good prose!", or in cant, "Communicate!" Such advice is bracing but not very helpful. Clarity depends on many things besides an agile syntax, a good ear, and the brevity that sires so much besides wit.

Familiarity, more than any other one thing, would seem to determine clarity. Clarity's model of models, the prose of John Dryden, seems far from clear to a student whose prose reading has started at Thomas Hardy and soared to Ernest Hemingway. Conversely, a psychological report incomprehensible to me opens like a flower to a psychologist. "Translate into English" makes a good classroom rubric for such stuff but would be disastrous put into practice. It would never get published. The journal editor would think it unclear, thin, meager, unprofessional. Familarity means reassurance. Clarity's first job is to make us feel at home. We want to see where we are. And it is not simple familiarity of manner that we expect, but of content as well. When a politician meets the press, the situation keys us not simply to a manner of answer but a kind of answer. Vague, generalized, evasive, determined—at whatever cost to logic or history—not to offend, such answers are still "clear" enough in context: "No, I will not be trapped by that vote two years ago," "No, I will not offend the Blacks." In such a tedious environment only a direct answer (or an indirect question) could really perplex the viewer.

Psychologists interested in perception have, ever since the experiments of Adelbert Ames, known that we tend to perceive what we want to perceive. This, in turn, is conditioned by what we have already perceived and by the framework we have been taught to perceive in. We don't just see something "out there." Our perceptive apparatus conditions, filters out, focuses the raw data that initiate the process of seeing. So it is with prose styles. They are not neutral, dependable, preexistent objects that everyone sees the same way. We must be trained, as Americans for the most part are not, to see them at all. And to see them in the same way (this is what an education in "taste" really means) takes a good deal of training indeed.

Move the argument one step further. Each prose style is itself not only an object seen but a way of seeing, both an intermediate "reality" and a dynamic one. Obviously there can be no single verbal pattern that can be called "clear." All depends on context—social, historical, attitudinal.

Clarity, then, like style in the American architect Thomas Hasting's definition, is "the job done." And it will, in this expanded sense, be achieved only by sensitivity to social situation and verbal surface in their many interrelationships. Exhortation gets you nowhere. When you say "Be clear!" to an indignant adolescent writing a silly letter to a college newspaper which is, if possible, sillier than he, you are really not saying anything about prose. You are saying, "Think straight!" "Try out a little evidence!" "Feel pressures other than those you feel!"—above all, "Grow up!" The prose has indeed revealed these moral inadequacies, but if the moral inadequacies trouble you, address yourself to those and not to the prose. A sense of style does enable you to detect "as in a flash, pretentious, slovenly, inadequate expressions which are the outcome of vain, lazy, or crooked thoughts" (Simeon Potter, *Language in the Modern World*, p. 11), but you do not gain the sense of style by being good, working hard, and thinking straight. Verbal awareness, not moral exhortation, finds the way to clarity in prose. America has the exhortation in full supply but hardly the awareness. Perhaps this explains our prose problem.

No absolute norm of "clarity" prevails, then, just as no absolute norm of prose does. No particular choice or configuration of words can pattern perfection. Nor can we judge prose by the scientific precision with which it transmits concepts, since most prose transmits feelings and attitudes, unstated assumptions and embarrassing implications, as well as concepts. When we use words, we use signs. And, as Morse Peckham has pointed out in *Man's Rage for Chaos* (p. 90), "In examining signs we are perforce within the sign field and cannot get out. Ultimately, to perceive is to *choose, will, intend.*"

Coleridge defined style as nothing but the clear expression of the meaning. This is fine so long as our definition of clarity and meaning remains broad. Is, then, no prose good or bad but success or failure make it so? The repugnance such a conclusion calls up should reveal more than it has. It means our response is fundamentally aesthetic rather than informational, formal rather than semantic. Good prose, clear prose, is finally an affair of form not of conceptual clarity. It works by pleasing us. As Henri Delacroix says at one point in *Le Langage et La Pensée (Language and Thought)*:

Le language est jusqu'à un certain point, comme la magie, une technique née du désir, qui assure au désir sa réalisation par des moyens nés du désir.

[Language, up to a point, is like magic, a technique engendered by desire, one which assures desire its realization by means born of desire.]

At the base of prose style, then, we find not only the need to communicate but the spirit of play, the delight in form for

its own sake. A zeal to inform has in our time bleached out
this delight, but we should not therefore confuse the two.
"Prose," one treatise tells us, "has mainly if not entirely a
descriptive function." Turn this advice upside down. Description describes only a small part of what prose does.
Find its true center of gravity, not in a faithful rendering of
Our Inmost Thoughts, or of A Rainy Day at Camp (to
borrow from The Books), but in the regularity with which it
pleases us. Clarity, like The Books' other shibboleth,
persuasion, is not an act of logic but an act of charm.

Let us try to sustain this surprising thesis with examples.
Look at a recent model of and monument to clarity, the
New English Bible. Here, in this new translation, Matthew 7
begins:

Pass no judgments and you will not be judged. For as you judge
others, so you will yourselves be judged, and whatever measure
you deal out to others will be dealt back to you. Why do you look
at the speck of sawdust in your brother's eye, with never a thought
for the great plank in your own? Or how can you say to your
brother, "Let me take the speck out of your eye," when all the
time there is that plank in your own? You hypocrite! First take
the plank out of your own eye, and then you will see clearly to
take the speck out of your brother's.

Do not give dogs what is holy; do not throw your pearls to the
pigs: they will only trample on them, and turn and tear you to
pieces.

The new translation's one, indeed only, avowed purpose is
clarity. The King James Version is hard to follow. The most
familiar Book has now become the least familiar. The
stylistic opacity of Elizabethan English has to be cleared up,
along with manifest translational errors of sense and
emphasis. In these terms, we applaud. Devout or not, you
get the message and get it quick. Sawdust, plank, pigs, you
see right through the words to the moral lesson beneath.
The King James (1611) Version does not nearly so well:

Judge not, that ye be not judged. For with what judgment ye
judge, ye shall be judged: and with what measure ye mete, it shall

be measured to you again. And why beholdest thou the mote that is in thy brother's eye? Or how wilt thou say to thy brother, "Let me pull out the mote out of thine eye"; and, behold, a beam is in thine own eye? Thou hypocrite, first cast out the beam out of thine own eye; and then shalt thou see clearly to cast out the mote out of thy brother's eye.

Give not that which is holy unto the dogs, neither cast ye your pearls before swine, lest they trample them under their feet, and turn again and rend you.

Not so clear. "Beam" for "plank," "mote" for "speck," "cast" for "take," "rend" for "tear." The diction perplexes. We raise pigs not swine. Pronoun usage differs. The Elizabethan translation uses a pleonasm "trample them under their feet" which the modern translation cleans up to "trample." Is the modern translation better prose? Better prose for the purpose?

Finally, neither. The *NEB* has purchased its conceptual, or perhaps we should say narrative, clarity at the expense of life and personality. Its prose is committee prose. It has no style. Always clear but never memorable, it fails to please. Why? Its alliteration is unintentional ("trample . . . turn . . . tear, pearls . . . pigs"), the older version's ("beholdest, brother's beam"; "measure, make, mote") is part of meaning-pattern. The *NEB* translator has, for clarity, avoided pronounced rhythm. Thus the Elizabethan allows himself five "judges" instead of four, makes us see the repetition as a pattern. He carefully repeats the rhythm of "for with what judgment ye judge, ye shall be judged" in the second half of the sentence. The reciprocity he is *talking about* is reflected by the rhythm and syntax of the sentence. He allows himself the negative imperative "Give not" to echo the "Judge not" that begins the passage. The similarity draws the two injunctions closer together as the *NEB* version does not. The syntax of the last sentence is clearer, but at the expense of the climactic structure that lends such stress to *rend* and indeed justifies so strong a word.

The Elizabethan translator has tried, too, to be clear, but natural to the kind of prose he wrote came an effort to please, to please by patterns of sound-arrangement and rhythm. Such devices of the verbal surface may be called ornament, but ornament integral to the prose sense, sense as meaning, entire effect. Is not part of clarity for a holy text its memorability? And does this not inevitably involve sound and rhythm? Church is one of the few places left where prose is read aloud. What we might profanely call the circumstances of performance demand a translation full of the sound and syntax patterns the King James Version supplies naturally because, at that time, prose was still regularly read aloud. The inadvertent alliteration of the *NEB*'s "pearls to the pigs," on the other hand, just makes us giggle. The pious often object to reading the Bible as literature, preferring to concentrate on what is seriously called "the message." Perhaps we are now in a position to see how mistaken such an objection is. The prose style creates the message, expressing, not merely enhancing, it. Scriptural prose owes fidelity beyond the biblical narrative to the whole of the religious experience. Here the joylessness of the *NEB* renders it—faithful translation as it is—unfaithful to the gospel spirit, deep, rich, rejoicing. The Christ of the *NEB* emerges a clear, cold, lifeless pedant.

Such a comparison as we've made is unfair, of course. The Authorized Version has been sanctified by time, rendered familiarly central to the Western mind. But isn't this what a religious text should be? You cannot *write* prose thus endowed but, endowment bestowed, it will embody the religious experience more than any new translation ever can. As a scripture, it will inevitably be clearer. Conversely, you can write a prose, flat, lifeless, neutral, scientifically clear, which *can never be remembered*. This is what the *NEB* translators have created. "Clarity" has here proved a disastrous criterion for prose style. The American architect Frank Lloyd Wright once drew a distinction much to our purpose. "Plainness," he said, "although simple, is not what I mean by simplicity. Simplicity is a clean, direct expression of that essential quality of the thing which is the nature of the thing itself." The new *NEB* translation is plain; the King James attains simplicity. Clarity is simple, not plain.

If clarity indicates a successful relationship between reader and writer, pleasure makes part of the success. The Books caution us repeatedly to remember the audience. But the pleasure in good prose will presumably be there for writer as well as reader. A writer may write for his own pleasure, less from zeal to communicate than from love for words. Furthermore, style will influence *what* a writer "wants" to say. People want to say what they are good at saying, can say most gracefully. The Books imply a one-time-process psychology of authorship. The spirit moves me to speak. I search for words, put proper words in proper places, do justice to the concept beneath. But this simplistic model does violence to both human motives and the power of words. Simple communication as motive will prevail only when all men are good and all things well. Even if I pick up my pen pure in heart, words cajole me. If I succeed in saying what I think, I rejoice because the act of writing has, in a sense, told me, made me see, what I think. The old Oscar Wilde jibe, "How do I know what I think until I hear what I say?" is literally true. Even purely expository prose less describes a truth than reveals one. The Books warn that idea-in-mind must always precede pen-in-hand. And we must always revise. Don't the two contradict each other? Our idea is clarified in the writing. We then think again, the idea before us. Words form idea. Then the reverse. This becomes a process, not a one-time event. Ernst Cassirer cautions in *The Logic of the Humanities* (p. 113): "It is never a question of imparting information, but of statement and response. It is only in this twofold process that true thought emerges."

Another of The Books' dogmas is "Control words! Don't

let them control you!" However, clarity as a process rather than a one-time relationship would seem to indicate a relationship between words and writer more complex than this. The writer controls words. Then they, as his first draft, control him. He then again, as revisor, controls them. *Da capo.* Clarity, then, as ever closer approximation of sentence to concept, involves a surrender to words as well as a victory over them. We can see here one of The Books' fundamental errors. They use a static, rather than a dynamic, model of verbal composition. It is not entirely true that ideas matter and words don't. It is not entirely true that you have not really had an idea until you've expressed it in words. Both are half-truths, stages of a process. In Western philosophy's long-standing quarrel between idealism and realism, The Books remain realists. Reality is "out there" and words must remain loyal to it.

A complete theory of prose style need not settle this endless dispute. But it should chart the whole dispute. It should account for a prose loyal to a preexistent reality and it should account for a prose loyal to words themselves as a final reference point. For the act of composition, as we have just seen, employs both perspectives, oscillates from realism to idealism and back again. Clarity, as a prose ideal, alternates a faith in things with a faith in words. The Books omit half the process. They thus ground themselves on both a false theory of knowledge and a false theory of perception. They assume both a neutral observer whom psychology has long ago disproved and a neutral language that even science has now discarded. Custom distinguishes expository prose from creative or fictional. The language of fiction, as David Lodge has made clear in a book of this name, cannot be judged by its fidelity to a preexisting reality. It creates the things it describes and thus cannot be anything *but* faithful. Clarity in prose keeps faith to just such a created reality. If we make a spectrum with the King James's Matthew passage at one end and a telegram ("Uncle

George died Mon Stop Funeral Wed Stop Come") at the other, we can say the whole spectrum is clear, but that most prose will tend to fall toward the Matthew end, true less to circumstance than to the inner logic of its own form. It will always try, that is, to suffuse fidelity-to-concept with pleasure, to inform it with attitude.

The impulse to do this shows up everywhere. When a World War II aircraft pilot radios back to his ship "Sighted sub, sunk same," he has at heart a message about himself as well as about the submarine. He wants to tell us *in what spirit* he sank the submarine, how he felt about his accomplishment. Such laconic insouciance has been created by his style. Alliteration, like rhyming and pun, is fun in itself, taking us, as Freud points out, back to a childhood where words were senseless, pure oral pleasure. Here the pilot's joy in his accomplishment shines drolly through the childish sound-play. He can afford the high spirits, the uncontrolled play because his deed implies a countervailing discipline. We thus uncover an irony. The theory of prose as a *descriptive* medium, neutral, denotative, is willing to sacrifice pleasure for clarity. Might it be that clarity finally *depends* on pleasure? That it embraces artifice rather than abandoning it? Prose, this argument leads us to assert, can never be forced into neutral statement for long. It always resists this pressure, and rightly. It wants to escape back to the eloquence—the poetry—from which it came. In doing so, it flees not to excrescent ornament but to its natural home. We might invert the classical relationship between the two. A traditional theorist argues:

All the qualities of good style may be ranged under two heads, perspicuity and ornament. For all that can possibly be required of language is, to convey our ideas clearly to the minds of others and, at the same time, in such a dress, as by pleasing and interesting them, shall most effectively strengthen the impressions which we seek to make. [Hugh Blair, Lecture 10 of *Lectures on Rhetoric and Belles Lettres*]

Instead, think of ornament, pure pleasure in pure form, as the center, and the ideas conveyed as clever enough to hitch a ride on the vehicle of delight.

Let us test these speculations about attitude on the norm itself, Dryden's prose. Here he begins the *Preface to Fables, Ancient and Modern*:

'Tis with a poet, as with a man who designs to build, and is very exact, as he supposes, in casting up the cost beforehand, but, generally speaking, he is mistaken in his account, and reckons short of the expense he first intended. He alters his mind as the work proceeds, and will have this or that convenience more, of which he had not thought when he began. So has it happened to me; I have built a house, where I intended but a lodge; yet with better success than a nobleman, who, beginning with a dog kennel, never lived to finish the palace he had contrived.

A well-known discussion of prose style lays it down "quite generally that the use of metaphor tends to obscure the essential nature of prose because it substitutes a poetic equivalence for a direct statement." Dryden begins with an extended simile between the poet and the man who builds, and then embraces the simile as a metaphor: "I have built a house, where I intended but a lodge." Further, he has built upon the relation of simile to metaphor the rhetorical *gradatio* (climax) that furnishes the structure for his opening paragraph. He opens with the initial comparison, then spells it out; casting the account, reckoning short, altering his mind, more conveniences. Then a transition, "So it has happened to me," prepares us for the climactic metaphor, "I have built a house, where I intended but a lodge." The opening structure ends with an illustrative anecdote, itself metaphorical, which invites us to ponder—and modify—the basic metaphor. The first section of the *Preface* aims to describe the genesis of the *Fables*. Dryden, starting humbly, built more largely than he intended, but did not, like the nobleman, start *meanly* upon a grandiose purpose. Nor, like him, has he failed to finish his design, enlarged though it be.

Dryden does not worry this opening metaphor to death but he does, in what follows, build on it. The house is given a family, the family of English poets, and these have their generations, of which Dryden is one. The metaphor stands as reference point and illustrative touchstone for what follows. Thus clarity in its real sense, a carefully orchestrated reader-writer relationship, here *begins* with metaphor, and in a fairly complex way. Dryden does not invite us to pause and ponder as I have done. But this does not mean he has not contrived his "clarity" carefully. You can see it in the syntax, which follows his thought, like the housemaker's purpose, as it proceeds in its unpremeditated turnings. " 'Tis with . . . and . . . as he supposes . . . but . . . and . . . So has it . . . yet with." The prose re-creates, in a model, how Dryden's mind had moved in creating the book. The Books, of course, permit none of this metaphorical hanky-panky. They would rewrite it something like this: "I did not intend, at first, to write so long a book." Dryden's far more poetic clarity breaks all the rules for being clear. Dryden remains, furthermore, wedded to this metaphorical strategy. Here is a later passage from the *Preface*:

With this account of my present undertaking I conclude the first part of this discourse: in the second part, as at a second sitting, tho' I alter not the draught, I must touch the same features over again, and change the dead-colouring of the whole.

He thus summarizes the self-portraiture of himself as old and infirm that had immediately preceded this graceful transition, and also prepares for the defense of himself and his method of translation that follows. He wants the picture of himself as old, worn, yet vigorous to stay in his reader's eye. He chooses again, as in the opening paragraph, the illustrative anecdote, the picture.

I leave them ["some original papers of my own"] wholly to the mercy of the reader. I will hope the best, that they will not be

condemned, but if they should, I have the excuse of an old
gentleman, who, mounting on horseback before some ladies, when
I was present, got up somewhat heavily, but desired of the fair
spectators that they would count fourscore and eight before they
judged him. By the mercy of God, I am already come within
twenty years of his number, a cripple in my limbs, but what
decays are in my mind, the reader must determine.

How cleverly the anecdote puts us just where Dryden wants
us. If we criticize his book, we are like a young lady
laughing at a venerable octogenarian.

Dryden's prose in the *Preface* remains, in fact, metaphorical throughout. Not only does he repeatedly refer to the
"thread of his discourse," but his "verses swell," Virgil
warms him by degrees, Homer sets him on fire all at once,
the English poets become a family with, as father, a
Chaucer who was "a little dipt in the rebellion of the
Commons." Anecdote and digression, proverb and quotation, easy conversational—almost associational—syntax, a
reflectional restatement and self-questioning which casts the
reader in his implied role in the *Preface*'s argument—all
these build a contrived, artificial prose. Plain statement,
meaning pure and semantic, "that absolute precision of
statement which is the mark of excellent prose," supply but
the beginning of Dryden's purpose. Such prose as he writes
aims above all at *tone,* creating a certain reader-writer
relationship. And this relationship remains drenched in
qualities, emotions, attitudes. The clarity it attains is Frank
Lloyd Wright's simplicity, form and purpose congruent. If
Dryden is the model of English prose, then prose provides
the vehicle of *attitude* as much as of statement or description.
Dryden's prose works in this world not, as The Books
recommend, in the next.

3 The Opaque Style

My theory has always been that the public will accept style, provided you do not call it style either in words or by, as it were, standing off and admiring it.

Raymond Chandler Speaking, p. 61

Prose style knows but a single taxonomy: the classification into high, middle, and low. That this has lasted with little protest from Cicero's day to our own demonstrates its flexibility more than its precision, but any explanation of the Expository Prose Vision Moralized must pass through it to a more satisfactory categorization. The threefold division emerges from an earlier one, earlier in logic as well as time: thought will demand one style, emotion another. Thought will find a style that is logical, clear, unornamental, largely unpatterned. Emotion will devise a different strategy, appealing through form and stock response rather than through clarity and logic. These set down two poles: teach thinking and move feeling. An intermediate position pops up like a mushroom. It will do something of both. Argue with feeling, move with logic.

These three positions form the basis for several discriminations. We discriminate by purposes: reason with in the low style, move in the high, or "conciliate" (as Cicero calls it) by some combination. Or we separate by subject: high style for serious subject, low for humble tasks of ordering life, middle for the mixed world between or small subject that promises greatly. But neither purpose nor subject tells us about the style itself, the pattern of words. Three additional specific criteria can animate the threefold division: syntax, diction, density of ornament. The high style chooses specialized or unfamiliar or highly resonant words and puts them into careful patterns of balance, antithesis, and climax. It allows itself the ornaments of sound (alliteration, assonance, rhyme), puns, the whole range of metaphor and simile, the pleasures of repetition and restatement. The low style uses none of these; the middle style, some, but moderately and in moderate combination.

Such a tripartite scheme contains its paradoxes. At moments of great stress or significance, the flattest cliché, the most obviously "low" of low styles, can take on supreme dignity—so Lear, when he meets the returned Cordelia:

> Pray, do not mock me:
> I am a very foolish fond old man,
> Fourscore and upward, not an hour more nor less;
> And, to deal plainly,
> I fear I am not in my perfect mind.

[4.7.59–63]

We can moralize the three stages. The high style, whatever its syntax, diction, or logical appeal, will be that style which "achieves a vision of society which draws speaker and hearers together into a closer bond." "It is," Northrop Frye continues in *The Well-Tempered Critic* (p. 44), "the voice of the genuine individual reminding us of our genuine selves, and of our role as members of a society, in contrast to a mob." This style moves the audience, but it includes its antithesis, the style that teaches them. Frye unites the two purposes that classical antiquity had seen as disparate. He builds his transcendence on imagination, the unity of thought and feeling. This unity is the high style's effect on the audience. Effect thus finally defines style. The concomitant definition, which Frye goes on to describe (pp. 45–46), proceeds from the moral purpose of the speaker.

High style in ordinary speech is heard whenever a speaker is honestly struggling to express what his society, as a society, is trying to be and do. It is even more unmistakably heard, as we should expect, in the voice of the individual facing a mob, or some incantation of the mob spirit, in the death speech of Vanzetti, in Joseph Welch's annihilating rebuke of McCarthy during the

McCarthy hearings, in the dignity with which a New Orleans mother explained her reasons for sending her white child to an unsegregated school. All these represent in different ways the authority of high style in action, moving, not on the middle level of thought, but on the higher level of imagination and social vision.

It is such careful thinking and brilliant example as this which underlies the mechanical call for sincerity in books on prose style. Yet offered even so ably, such a definition presents problems. Sincerity wears many masks. Few of us speak all our minds all the time, thank Heaven. The "genuine self" of which Frye speaks is, literally, an act of faith. And how do we judge "the closer bond" produced by a genuine high style? "Such style has a peculiar quality of penetration about it: it elicits a shock of recognition, as it is called, which is the proof of its genuineness." What help is this? Just as the scientific criterion for prose, conceptual clarity, demands a preexisting concept to be clear about, so the moral criterion for prose implies a morality to be true to. No morality, no shock of recognition. Frye has little patience for the "high style = ornamental style" equation: "High style in this sense is emphatically not the high-flown style: all ornate language in rhetoric belongs to the middle style, the language of society engaged in routine verbal ritual." The real criteria for the high style must be moral, not aesthetic.

The trouble with the tripartite division is not that it is vague and thus inapplicable. It is so vague it is nearly always applicable—especially so if you redefine it thoroughly, either morally or affectively. You can even adapt it to the dictates of clarity and scientific prose. The high style becomes bad, the middle good, and the low "colloquial." No, the trouble lurks in the tripartite division itself. Because it renders comparison invidious, it introduces the dispute that invidious comparison inevitably brings. It cannot just describe, it must evaluate. Which purposes are best? Which subjects most serious? Who, what, most moral? More than this, it has repeatedly proved itself tone-deaf. It can tell you what was said and explain why it was said that way, but it seldom reveals the *spirit* in which it was said. It defines badly the kind of agreement struck between writer and reader. It forces us, finally, to take an attitude toward style, whether the attitude be formal (diction, syntax, density of figures), moral (as with Frye's definition), or scientific. It asks us, in the composition course, to teach things that cannot be taught.

Since no other categorization has ever been offered, one must be devised. Instead of a hierarchical, vertical metaphor, picture a horizontal one—a spectrum. Instead of three "steps" or "styles," allow an infinite number. Instead of morality, effect on the audience, conceptual clarity or ornament, try to measure a psychological variable, stylistic self-consciousness. To what degree does a writer acknowledge his style *as a style?* To what degree are we to *feel* the style as such? To what degree, that is, does the style realize itself as opaque, as—the enemy of clarity—a style to be looked *at* rather than *through?* Finally, what implications for prose style, and for the teaching of prose style, does such a categorization bring?

Here are three exemplary styles. The high-middle-low nomenclature yields results very different from the opaque style spectrum. First, a passage from Hemingway's *A Farewell to Arms*:

The waiter brought a dish of sauerkraut with a slice of ham over the top and a sausage buried in the hot wine-soaked cabbage. I ate it and drank the beer. I was very hungry. I watched the people at the table in the cafe. At one table they were playing cards. Two men at the table next me were talking and smoking. The cafe was full of smoke. The zinc bar, where I had breakfasted, had three people behind it now; the old man, a plump woman in a black dress who sat behind a counter and kept track of everything served to the tables, and a boy in an apron. I wondered how many children the woman had and what it had been like.

When I was through with the *choucroute* I went back to the hospital. The street was all clean now. There were no refuse cans out. The day was cloudy but the sun was trying to come through. I rode upstairs in the elevator, stepped out and went down the hall to Catherine's room, where I had left my white gown. I put it on and pinned it in back at the neck. I looked in the glass and saw myself looking like a fake doctor with a beard. I went down the hall to the delivery room. The door was closed and I knocked. No one answered so I turned the handle and went in. The doctor sat by Catherine. The nurse was doing something at the other end of the room.

"Here is your husband," the doctor said.

By aesthetic criteria, this is surely the low style: no ornament, no word-play, a commonplace choice of words, above all, syntactic simplicity, almost exclusively simple and compound sentences. Effect on the audience? Low style again. The novelist deliberately avoids playing on our feelings. Dignity of subject? Low style again, for the passage deals with ordinary experience. The morality criterion seems impossible to apply here.

Now a passage in the middle style, a selection from Somerset Maugham's essayistic intellectual autobiography, *The Summing Up*:

For to write good prose is an affair of good manners. It is, unlike verse, a civil art. Poetry is baroque. Baroque is tragic, massive and mystical. It is elemental. It demands depth and insight. I cannot but feel that the prose writers of the baroque period, the authors of King James's Bible, Sir Thomas Browne, Glanville, were poets who had lost their way. Prose is a rococo art. It needs taste rather than power, decorum rather than inspiration and vigour rather than grandeur. Form for the poet is the bit and the bridle without which (unless you are an acrobat) you cannot ride your horse; but for the writer of prose it is the chassis without which your car does not exist. It is not an accident that the best prose was written when rococo with its elegance and moderation, at its birth attained its greatest excellence. For rococo was evolved when baroque had become declamatory and the world, tired of the stupendous, asked for restraint. It was the natural expression of persons who valued a civilized life. Humour, tolerance and horse sense made the great tragic issues that had preoccupied the first half of the seventeenth century seem excessive. The world was a more comfortable place to live in and perhaps for the first time in centuries the cultivated classes could sit back and enjoy their leisure. It has been said that good prose should resemble the conversation of a well-bred man. Conversation is only possible when men's minds are free from pressing anxieties. Their lives must be reasonably secure and they must have no grave concern about their souls. They must attach importance to the refinements of civilization. They must value courtesy, they must pay attention to their persons (and have we not also been told that good prose should be like the clothes of a well-dressed man, appropriate but unobtrusive?), they must fear to bore, they must be neither flippant nor solemn, but always apt; and they must look upon "enthusiasm" with a critical glance. This is a soil very suitable for prose.

A style calculated to convey information, this. The civilized style of the English essay that Maugham is talking about, he also illustrates. His prose embodies the middle style par excellence. It does not offer the calculated simplicity of diction and syntax that Hemingway chose, yet it doesn't fetch words from afar either. Nobody would think the syntax contrived. An important subject is described but not a great one. It both discusses good manners and displays them in its open, easy, yet not informal address to the reader, one appropriate but unobtrusive.

Now here is a third passage, from a contemporary novel by James Gould Cozzens, *By Love Possessed*:

Accepting the filled sherry glass, Julius Penrose took a swallow. "This unhappy event has several unhappy aspects," he said. "Well, we owe nature a death, I'm told. By our choosing to be born, we contracted for death. Recision would be inequitable and unjust. Let me hear no more complaining! The terms of payment? Not exorbitant, I think. What could be more generous? If we pay this year, we won't have to pay next year." He took another sip of sherry. "Regarding the dead, our pious rule is nothing if not good. Ralph, let us agree, is a little bastard; and you won't suppose I mean by the term that Alice Detweiler could have ever had the appetite, let alone the imagination, to play George false. Helen is known to have been faithful and true, good and self-sacrificing, and, perhaps not so relevant, but they are qualities in the main admired, chaste and pure. She is, therefore, virtue; Ralph is vice. Because of all this virtue, Helen's sorrows, her sufferings, the last full measure of her rash act, put her publicly, in terms of public opinion, unassailably in the right. Everybody must feel that."

Julius Penrose took a sip of sherry. "Yes; I too feel it; but do I think it? An entrance is won to the heart; but to the head? Passion and reason, self-division's cause! I'm afraid I think that this gentle and unspotted soul was and is, has been and now always will be, very much in the wrong. On people as people, I try never to pass judgment—we can seldom know what the real truth about them is. Yet on acts, acts of theirs, I see no reason to hesitate in passing judgment—this is good; this is bad; this is mean; this is kind. On such points, I'm competent, as every man is. Like the common law, we secular moralists aren't interested in the why; we observe the what. Here, the what that gives me pause is this. Ralph's a little bastard; yes. Something ought to have been done to and about him, I'd think preferably with a horsewhip, if nowadays one could be found. Be good, or I'll beat you! That's in order. That's fair warning and fair play. Could the same be said of a verbal threat to do a thing like this—Ralph must be good, or Helen will kill herself? And how much less, if, for mere threat, performance is substituted? No; there is a want of principle, which is to say, too much feeling. I pronounce this bad. I pronounce this mean. The sentence, of course, is on the act, not the person. I pity the person; I take her to be mad, possessed by love. Her feelings acted. Here is simply more of feeling's comic or tragic, yet, to the feeler, always juicy, fruits. I quote: 'A warmth within the breast would melt the freezing reason's colder part. And like a man in wrath, the heart stood up and answered: I have felt!' Let us pass on. Your refection is spread; take some."

Within the traditional categories, the style is high. The
subject is serious, the occasion climactic. The reader's
feelings are carefully enlisted by a series of verbal artifices.
A special legal diction, for example, icy and remote
(recision, inequitable, pass judgment, competent, in order,
the sentence, I pronounce) contrasts with the situation's
macabre immediacy, a Helen who has drunk half a bottle of
cleaning fluid. Cozzens plans his sentences to have—and
show—the balance, antithesis, parenthesis, and climax
usually called "periodic":

Helen is known to have been faithful and true,

                                        good and self-sacrificing
        and (perhaps not so relevant, but
        they are qualities ((in the main))
        admired)

                                        chaste and pure.
        She is (therefore) virtue;
Ralph is   vice.

Cozzens develops a situation already resonant with literary
symbolism, a "refection," a ceremonial communion meal of
wafer and wine, and spices it with quotations, "Passion and
Reason, self-division's cause"; buried quotations, "the last
full measure of her rash act"; echoes of The Book of
Common Prayer, "was and is, has been and now always will
be"; proverbial allusion "our pious rule" (*nihil nisi bonum*);
and popular allusion, the "juicy fruits" of Juicy Fruit
chewing gum. He allows himself the kind of repetitive
elaboration, the savoring of a word by redefinition, that
older English prose was fond of: "publicly, in terms of
public opinion," "unhappy event . . . unhappy aspects."
Julius Penrose is given to that kind of reasoning-with-one-
self-aloud ("Let me hear no more complaining! The terms
of payment? Not exorbitant, I think. What could be more
generous?") which classical rhetoricians called *hypophora*.
We might even fit the passage into Frye's exclusive

definition of the high style, in spite of the verbal artifice. For Julius Penrose is very valiantly trying to express what he and Arthur Winner, and the society they constitute, really feel about the suicide, how sense is to be made of it.

We have, then, reasonable samples of the three styles as traditionally defined. (Two of the three are prose fiction; this raises problems to be considered later.) The process of categorizing tells us something about them but, distorting a good deal, ignores more. Placing them on a self-consciousness spectrum renders the invidious high-middle-low order oddly undescriptive. Posit the two extremes of our spectrum. Both are unliterary. At the extreme left, childish babble, nursery rhymes, pure pleasure in words. Words here are things. You play with them. They have shape, sound, corporeality. At the other end, a mathematical equation, pure significance, all sign. Pleasure flows from concepts. Nonsense rhyme presents a perfectly opaque surface, equations a perfectly transparent one. Between two such extremes all prose should embody a continuous spectrum. Scientific prose falls far toward the right, equation side; here Dryden and Swift, so mistakenly considered monuments to clarity, are glued down. Correspondingly, on the left we find the prose of *Finnegan's Wake*; a little further to the right, *Ulysses*; further, *Dubliners*. Maugham's prose, as in our example, lives and moves in the middle. But both Hemingway and Cozzens would occupy the same position, to the left of Maugham. In both, style is to be seen as such, symbolic opacity.

By fleeing the high style, Hemingway dramatizes a flight from everything it represents. His syntax stops with too studied a simplicity. It cautions us, by its very divergence from normative prose, to notice it as a syntax. So, too, does the style as a whole—diction, rhythm, tone—a low style that wants to be seen as a low style. Style stands in deliberate contrast to situation. Fredric Henry, under great pressure, endures the climax of his love for Catherine

Barkley just as we endure the climax of the novel. Hemingway intensifies the low style at this point. Why? To symbolize the hero's attitude toward the pressure. The style—deliberate, maximally controlled, utterly plain— symbolizes, indeed creates the heroism. The act of stylistic control stands for the controlled feelings the hero (and such control *is* his heroism) cannot express directly. Hemingway thus plays against the old tripartite stylistic expectancy. We expect a speech on stoic endurance of grief. He offers the opposite, a new kind of bravery.

We can see this only if we acknowledge the style as such, look *at it* and not *through it*. The opaque segment of the spectrum, by compelling this attention to surface, guides with more accuracy to the passage's center. Only attention to the stylistic surface yields the meaning it adumbrates—a meaning not beneath it but on it. By the canons of conceptual clarity, such a reflective surface stands triple-damned. In the words of James Sutherland (*On English Prose*, p. 28):

Style, of course, is not just a patina that gathers on the surface of old prose; but when we become too conscious of style it is either because the writer himself was too conscious of it while he was writing, or because his prose is already moribund and is beginning to give off the characteristic aroma of antiquity.

It should be clear by now how such a conception misleads. A writer cannot be, for a certain range of effects, too conscious of style or make us too conscious of it. Yet Cozzens has been called names for doing just this, just what has earned Hemingway his title of plain stylist. In the Cozzens passage, as with *A Farewell to Arms*, context reveals how the style works. Julius Penrose ends his homily with "Your refection is spread; take some." Here is what immediately follows:

"I'm not hungry," Arthur Winner said. "Julius, how long have you known that Noah's accounts were short?"

"Ah!" Julius Penrose said. "Well, I'm not sorry to have you ask! Yes: that's where I was putting off getting."

The whole "refection" speech, so carefully bounded by sherry at the beginning and biscuit at the end, functions as a digressive evasion of the hard business to be talked. The nice blend of periodic syntax and colloquiality that characterizes Julius Penrose is here only slightly exaggerated, but enough, with the concluding mention of "putting off," to tell us that he was making a speech and knew he was making a speech. The high style, indeed, fits the subject of the speech, but it becomes, given the fictional context, more than slightly ironical. Again, unless we can see the style as style, we shall go wide of its real function in the novel. Cozzens depends upon the three-style convention to illuminate his departure from it. His ironical, opaque high style needs a set of categories beyond high-middle-low, in other words, needs our spectrum.

The self-consciousness spectrum forces no preconceived attitudes upon us. Right is no higher than left. We need not judge the dignity of the subject, its decorum, its morality. Only a stylistic judgment is required. How should we attend to or "take" the style? Does it diminish into insignificance on the right or does it move left, growing so large in our consciousness as to become the subject? This is a fundamental question to ask about style, and the only one that does not force attitudinizing of one sort or another. It is possible, of course, to foist an attitude on the spectrum, most commonly the normative theorist's dislike of ornament. To this vagary, and to the spectrum's confutation of it, we must now turn.

The road of excess may lead to the palace of wisdom, as Blake asseverated, but for prose few have thought so. Stylistic excess has been suspect and scorned since Aristotle, whose *Rhetoric* cautions against letting style and persuasion show. The intended victims are put on guard, start patting their pockets. So, too, a style that seems oversize or unnecessary to the meaning is condemned. A famous critic asserts: "Style occurs in isolation only when it is bad, when it fails to coincide with meaning" (W. K. Wimsatt, *The Prose Style of Samuel Johnson*, p. 10). This style for the sake of style Americans usually call "rhetoric," or verbal pyrotechnics. Opposite to rhetoric, the perfect union of thought and word falls well to the right in the spectrum; for only by detaching style from meaning can we see it as a self-conscious style.

Rhetoric is the opposite of the process which I have called crystalization. Instead of condensing your emotion upon the cause, which becomes the symbol; instead of defining and making concrete your thought, by the aid of your sensuous perception; you give way to a mere verbal exaggeration of your feeling or your thought. [Murry, *The Problem of Style*, p. 118]

Such a distinction depends on the scientific attitude toward prose: all prose cherishes an object outside itself, a concept it must embody. When the language starts to cloud, it goes bad. But on the opaque-style spectrum, which does not render attitudinizing verdicts, it does not. It simply shifts its loyalty elsewhere, shifts it increasingly to the words themselves. Style *becomes* subject. You cannot then insist it ought to serve its subject. This, precisely, it does. Confront as example what has long been recognized as the most extreme stylistic extravagance, the most outrageous literary rhetoric in English, John Lyly's 1574 *Euphues, The Anatomy of Wit*. Here is a brief sample, but there are a hundred pages just like it. Euphues and his friend Philautus are slugging it out in an ordinary Euphuistic chat:

Euphues had continual access to the place of Philautus and no little familiarity with him; and finding him at convenient leisure, in these short terms unfolded his mind unto him:

"Gentleman and friend, the trial I have had of thy manners cutteth off divers terms which to another I would have used in the like matter. And since a long discourse argueth folly, and delicate words incur the suspicion of flattery, I am determined to use neither of them, knowing either of them to breed offense. Weighing with myself the force of friendship by the effects, I studied ever since my first coming to Naples to enter league with such a one as might direct my steps, being a stranger, and resemble my manners, being a scholar; the which two qualities as I find in you able to satisfy my desire, so I hope I shall find a heart in you willing to accomplish my request. Which if I may obtain, assure yourself that Damon to his Pythias, Pylades to his Orestes, Titus to his Gysippus, Theseus to his Pirithous, Scipio to his Laelius, was never found 'more faithful than Euphues will be to Philautus."

Philautus by how much the less he looked for this discourse, by so much the more he liked it, for he saw all qualities both of body and mind in Euphues; unto whom he replied as followeth:

"Friend Euphues—for so your talk warranteth me to term you—I dare neither use a long process, neither a loving speech, lest unwittingly I should cause you to convince me of those things which you have already condemned. And verily I am bold to presume upon your courtesy, since you yourself have used so little curiosity, persuading myself that my short answer will work as great an effect in you as your few words did in me. And seeing that we resemble, as you say, each other in qualities, it cannot be that the one should differ from the other in courtesy. Seeing the sincere affection of the mind cannot be expressed by the mouth and that no art can unfold the entire love of the heart, I am earnestly to beseech you not to measure the firmness of my faith by the fewness of my words, but rather think that the overflowing waves of good will leave no passage for many words. Trial shall prove trust. Here is my hand, my heart, my lands, and my life at thy commandment. Thou mayest well perceive that I did believe thee that so soon I did love thee, and I hope thou wilt the rather love me in that I did believe thee."

Either Euphues and Philautus stood in need of friendship or were ordained to be friends. Upon so short warning to make so soon a conclusion might seem, in mine opinion, if it continued, miraculous; it shaken off, ridiculous.

This is a typical passage. Others intensify these ornamental tricks. It is easy to see why scholars condemn the work with a puzzlement akin to religious wonder. But we might describe before we deplore. Antithetical balance and parallelism of all sorts scream the loudest.

> direct my steps, being a stranger
> resemble my manners, being a scholar
> neither a long process—neither a long speech
> firmness of my faith—fewness of my words
> so short a warning—so soon a conclusion

Alliteration and assonance (beginning word rhyme) point to themselves repeatedly, especially in words occupying similar places in balanced or parallel constructions: folly / flattery; force of friendship; looked for / liked it; long process / loving speech; firmness of my faith; so short / as soon; my hand / my heart; my lands / and my life. And sometimes words that sound alike are put in similar places to draw them into antithesis:

And verily I am bold to presume upon your *courtesy*
since you yourself have used so little *curiosity*

Lyly dotes on proverbs ("Trial shall prove trust") though not so much in this passage as elsewhere. He likes to build a climax:

1. Here is my hand
2. my heart
3. my lands
4. and my life
5. at thy commandment.

Notice here how the alliterative patterns of hand / heart and lands / life intersect the climactic structure and change the hand, lands, heart, life order which would supply the more usual scale of values. Similar endings often draw two words into antithesis: if it continued, miraculous; if shaken off, ridiculous. Occasionally Lyly will suspend the sense over a long, involved syntax that seems almost syllogistic:

Seeing the sincere affection of the mind cannot be
expressed by the mouth and that no art can unfold the entire
love of the heart
    I am earnestly to beseech you
                              not to measure the firmness of my
                              faith by the fewness of my words

The repetitions of single words and sometimes of phrases
needs no emphasis.

How to appraise such a style? The older classification
calls it a high style, but a bad one, written by a stylistic
compulsive. This has remained the common view. But in
terms of a stylistic spectrum that does not force its attitudes
on the reader how does such a style work? It makes us
acknowledge, as a first step, that Lyly wanted to interpose a
vivid stylistic self-consciousness between himself and his
readers—full left. Such self-conscious excess indicates an
equally self-conscious bid for attention. Verbal ornament, as
every Shakespearean playgoer knows, enchanted the Elizabethan of Lyly's time. Lyly's bid for attention will be a
virtuoso art. How far can a fairly limited · grab bag of
rhetorical tricks be carried? He will show them. *Euphues* did.
It constituted, for Lyly, an elaborate bid for employment.
He had no future. He wanted to become Revels Master.
The job needed a witty, clever man. He would show how
clever he was.

A style is a response to a situation. When you call a style
bad, or exaggerated, much less mad, you ought to make
sure you understand the situation it responds to. You may
be objecting to the situation, not to the style invented to
cope with it. So here. We object to the love of ornament, of
words for their own sake, which engendered such extravagant verbal frivolity. And we object to a rhetorical show-
piece consciously used as "advertisement for myself." We
object to its exhibitionism. We wish prose to assume other,
more familiar attitudes.

We might carry reflections on Euphuism and stylistic

excess a step further by examining a letter of Flaubert's (quoted in Kenneth Burke's *Counter-Statement*, p. 6), who inherited quite another climate of prose attitudes, but still saw clearly what Lyly only half-knew he was after.

What seems beautiful to me, what I should most like to do, would be a book about nothing, a book without any exterior ties, but sustained by the internal force of its style . . . a book which would have almost no subject, or at least in which the subject would be almost invisible, if that is possible. The most beautiful works are those with least matter.

Euphues goes on too long to be only a display-piece (in the old sense of the word, a "masterpiece"). It has a plot, but hardly one that matters—a prodigal-son moral a thousand times dead. Its characterization amounts to even less. It stands as the first document of English prose to view prose style with any attitude but the conceptual. Lyly is often damned as intoxicated. Well he might have been. He was the first to see new directions for prose and a new kind of relationship to his reader. He began to see that the logical development of prose would be from the conceptual or scientific attitude to the aesthetic or playful, from right spectrum to left.

His discovery came at the wrong time. England had just finished such a cycle in verse and a reaction was about to set in. It brought with it the prose of Dryden and Swift, and the scientific attitude toward prose. We have had to complete an entire cycle to return to an attitude toward prose similar to Lyly's. It appears all over the fictional landscape these days in America, but most cleverly in Vladimir Nabokov's novel *Ada*. *Ada* is *Euphues* redivivus.

How did the scuffle start? Did all three cross the brook stepping on slimy stones? Did Percy push Greg? Did Van jog Percy? Was there something—a stick? Twisted out of a fist? A wrist gripped and freed?

"Oho," said Percy, "you are playful, my lad!"

Greg, one bag of his plus-fours soaked, watched them help-
lessly—he was fond of both—as they grappled on the brink of the
brook.

Percy was three years older, and a score of kilograms heavier
than Van, but the latter had handled even burlier brutes with
ease. Almost at once the Count's bursting face was trapped in the
crook of Van's arm. The grunting Count toured the turf in a
hunched-up stagger. He freed one scarlet ear, was retrapped, was
tripped and collapsed under Van, who instantly put him "on his
omoplates," *na lopatki,* as King Wing used to say in his carpet
jargon. Percy lay panting like a dying gladiator, both shoulder
blades pressed to the ground by his tormentor, whose thumbs now
started to manipulate horribly that heaving thorax. Percy with a
sudden bellow of pain intimated he had had enough. Van
requested a more articulate expression of surrender, and got it.
Greg, fearing Van had not caught the muttered plea for mercy,
repeated it in the third person interpretive. Van released the
unfortunate Count, whereupon he sat up, spitting, palpating his
throat, rearranging the rumpled shirt around his husky torso and
asking Greg in a husky voice to find a missing cufflink.

Van washed his hands in a lower shelf-pool of the brook and
recognized, with amused embarrassment, the transparent tubular
thing, not unlike a sea-squirt, that had got caught in the
downstream course in a fringe of forget-me-nots, good name, too.

He had started to walk back to the picnic glade when a
mountain fell upon him from behind. With one violent heave he
swung his attacker over his head. Percy crashed and lay supine for
a moment or two. Van, his crab claws on the ready, contemplated
him, hoping for a pretext to inflict a certain special device of
exotic torture that he had not yet had the opportunity to use in a
real fight.

"You've broken my shoulder," grumbled Percy, half-rising and
rubbing his thick arm. "A little more self-control, young devil."

"Stand up!" said Van. "Come on, stand up! Would you like
more of the same or shall we join the ladies? The ladies? All right.
But, if you please, walk in front of me now."

As he and his captive drew near the glade Van cursed himself
for feeling rattled by that unexpected additional round; he was
secretly out of breath, his every nerve twanged, he caught himself

limping and correcting the limp—while Percy de Prey, in his magically immaculate white trousers and casually ruffled shirt, marched, buoyantly exercising his arms and shoulders, and seemed quite serene and in fact rather cheerful.

Presently Greg overtook them, bringing the cufflink—a little triumph of meticulous detection; and with a trite "Attaboy!" Percy closed his silk cuff, thus completing his insolent restoration.

Their dutiful companion, still running, got first to the site of the finished feast; he saw Ada, facing him with two stipple-stemmed red boletes in one hand and three in the other; and, mistaking her look of surprise at the sound of his thudding hooves for one of concern, good Sir Greg hastened to cry out from afar: "He's all right! He's all right, Miss Veen"—blind compassion preventing the young knight from realizing that she could not possibly have known yet what a clash had occurred between the beau and the beast.

"Indeed I am," said the former, taking from her a couple of her toadstools, the girl's favorite delicacy, and stroking their smooth caps. "And why shouldn't I be? Your cousin has treated Greg and your humble servant to a most bracing exhibition of Oriental Skrotomoff or whatever the name may be."

Scuffle, start, stepping, slimy stones, something, stick, twisted, fist, wrist? Here are the old figures of sound again, the "brink of the brook" and "burlier brutes," which brought the scorn of centuries down on Lyly. Here is the same self-conscious agreement to look at, admire, join in the game of, the verbal surface. The "third person interpretive" and *na lopatki* replace Lyly's classical allusions and proverbial citations, but the purpose stays the same—to intensify our awareness of style. Nabokov has always been a virtuoso but never more than here. The calculated artifice of the dialogue, the strange diction ("meticulous detection," "insolent restoration," "dutiful companion"), with its slight parodical echo of the chivalric "beau and the beast" archetype behind the passage, all invite not the breathless "Let me see life" attitude that scientific prose or realist fiction requires, but quite another. It says, rather, "How contrived, how literary, when it comes to that, most of our behavior is." The scientific stylist pictures a world where life as concepts comes first. The opaque stylist views experience differently: to him, life seems as stylized as literature. Ordinary experience seems fundamentally dramatic, a game of roles in which the self is not so much felt and possessed as presented and reenacted. For such an experience, the most faithful reflection will be a prose style equally contrived, literary, and self-conscious.

No one has, to my knowledge, criticized Nabokov for ornamental excess. This immunity may partly be explained by Nabokov's superior talent, or by the history of fiction separating him from Lyly. But it may also be because we now conceive of society, and of the self, in far more dramatic, literary terms than before. We perceive with less moral indignation the essential realism of the opaque style. The process that Lyly and Nabokov illustrate occurs pretty frequently, after all. "The artist's means," Burke tells us, "are always tending to become ends in themselves" (*Counter-Statement*, pp. 54–55). When such a tendency coincides, as now, with widespread, systematic doubt of the veracity of language itself, pressure for an opaque style intensifies. A writer who has given up on words as "meaningful" will use them as stage prop, as scene, as theater decoration, symbolic action, absurdist gesture.

Not an especially literary temptation, this. It holds for American advertising as well as for Lyly or his fellow Elizabethan, Thomas Nashe. The scientific attitude toward Lyly's prose aside, look whither his absurdist syntactic gestures tend. *Euphues*, from its prodigal-son theme to its compulsive antithesis, constitutes a plea for balance. Its "excessive" ornament embodies an eloquent cry for the balanced view of experience and self which Lyly could not sustain in his own life. So viewed, Lyly's ornament works as essentially in his fiction as Nabokov's does in his, though in a different way. For both, structural pattern indicates tone, the reference pattern of articulation that tells writer and reader how they stand. The prejudice against ornament invoked by the scientific attitude should not govern other attitudes. Attack ornament and you attack the imagination itself: "Any speculation regarding ornament is a speculation upon the great power of the abstract and upon the infinite resources of the imaginary" (Henri Focillon, *The Life of Forms in Art*, p. 19).

From one point of view, then, there is no such thing as excessive ornament in prose. We can never be, as the hero of an Elizabethan romance complains, poisoned with roses, unless the poisoning constitutes the main business at hand. The denser the ornament, the more manner becomes matter, style subject, words things. Within such an aesthetic, Swift's cozy "proper words in proper places" becomes meaningless. All words are proper words, and proper places are the places the opaque stylist carves out as proper. The cloying sense of Walter Pater's fulsome writing must not cloud a fundamental attitude toward prose. "Mannerism"—manner become subject—constitutes as legitimate an attitude as any other. To it the sober pieties of Swift, Arnold ("The needful qualities for a fit prose," he insists in "The Study of Poetry," "are regularity, uniformity, precision, balance"), and The Books simply do not apply. (The argument here could be amplified, of course. Swift's "proper words" formula constitutes an absurdly inadequate description of his own prose and Arnold's "needful qualities" hardly begin to describe Arnoldian prose.)

Up to now, I've not discriminated between fictional and nonfictional prose. One might think the discrimination crucial. As David Lodge has pointed out, fictional prose roams freer than exposition because it points to no preexisting reality but creates one instead. Take this thought a step further. The fiction / nonfiction distinction is really one of differences in attitude toward prose. Fiction can exploit the scientific attitude as well as exposition. The line of fiction

descending from Defoe uses expository prose. What difference does it make to prose stylists that Moll Flanders
never lived? Diarists who have lived inhabit the same
stylistic universe. Everything depends upon the prose attitude. As we can see by remembering the syllogistic Lyly
passage, even the form of a syllogism embodies an aesthetic
appeal, can be seen as opaque style, provided we are
prepared to invoke that attitude and not the scientific one.
Go a step further. Not only does the fiction / nonfiction
distinction prove false for prose style, but the literary / nonliterary one as well. The range of stylistics, under the
spectrum outlined, includes all verbal expression. Discriminate between literary and nonliterary and you have invoked the scientific attitude, admittedly or not. So René
Wellek writes:

Style may include all devices of speech that convey the attitude of
the speaker (all "expressive language") and all devices that aim to
achieve rhetorical ends, all devices for securing emphasis or
explicitness, metaphor, rhetorical figures, syntactical patterns.
Clearly, style embraces all speech and all writing. But stylistics as
part of a science of literature must be concerned with much more
special problems. [*Style in Language*, ed. T. A. Sebook, p. 417]

The scientific prejudice inheres in such an assertion, even in
trying to expel it. It seems clearer to distinguish two
attitudes toward style, scientific and opaque, than to
separate by conceptual referent into fictional and nonfictional.

The same confusion is often encountered when distin-
guishing poetry (or poetic prose) from prose (or "real"
prose, Dryden's prose). So Morton Bloomfield, in an essay
impressively titled "The Syncategorematic in Poetry" *(Essays and Explorations*, p. 267):

Poetic language calls attention to itself. . . . Poetic devices are the
artist's weapons in his fight against the transitivity of lexical words
[transitivity = outward references, words as "transparent"] . . .

When words lead to other words we are more conscious of their own wordhood than when they lead to concepts.

Here is the same confusion of attitudes. Nothing but confusion has ever come from the effort to fix the poetry-prose boundary. It seems easier, say, to isolate a scientific attitude toward prose that is also useful for some kinds of poetry. The opaque attitude proves useful for both. The stylistic spectrum, covering the whole range of expressivity from scientific to opaque, supplies an easier, more precise taxonomy than either fiction / exposition or prose / poetry. To say this only glosses Stendhal's definition of style: "Le style, c'est ajouter à une pensée donnée toutes les circon-stances propres à produire tout l'effet que doit produire cette pensée" [Style adds to a thought all the circumstances needed to produce the whole effect which that thought ought to produce]. Are we to commit ourselves to thought with the feeling-tones that surround it or without them? Doing without them, we move toward the right end of the spectrum; with them, we move toward the left, toward Stendhal's, and our, opaque style.

Some pedagogical implications emerge from this theo-rizing. The teaching of composition in America has been overpoweringly scientific and normative. But if we seek stylistic self-consciousness—and I see no other goal for a writing course in America now—not so much normative measurement as range of comparative exercises seems called for. The pattern of expectation created by continual normative measurement continually confuses, for it does not apply to anything students read, only to what they write. They read the great stylists, or pieces of them, and are told to imitate. But these worthies range all over the stylistic spectrum, from the chilly transparency of *In Cold Blood* to the venerable opacities of Sir Thomas Browne's "Urn-Burial." A normative, scientific attitude makes no sense for such a range of prose. Students, even slow ones, are not slow to see this. If both attitudes are to be taught, they ought to be made clear.

Instead, all the difficulties of the classical threefold scheme are introduced. A far more sensible procedure would dictate stylistic imitations such as an Elizabethan schoolboy did with his Vergil—imitate, compare student version and original, imitate again, compare once more—or the translation of one style into another. The role of ornament in teaching even the most neutral kind of scientific prose has never been discussed. Here is a student's reasonably successful attempt to, as The Books say, Be Clear:

The formal structures of Books I and III of *The Faerie Queene* represent two extremes of narrative planning. The story of Redcrosse, or Holinesse, consists of a well defined quest to be carried out by a single figure after he has been spiritually tested and prepared. Various characters impinge upon the central action, often placing obstacles for the completion of the task, and the routes travelled by Redcrosse and Una, together or separately, from the court of Gloriana to the castle of Una's parents, are certainly circuitous; nevertheless, the action in the book is well unified with an air of finality existing after the dragon's defeat, as symbolized by the betrothal of Holinesse and Truth. It would be hard to imagine a more complete distinction between the narrative features outlined above and those found in the Legend of Britomart, or Chastity. The latter depicts a knight whose major, if not only, reason for entering Fairy Land is her love, for Artegall. This motivation is mentioned early (Canto II) and then is virtually forgotten for the rest of the book. Indeed, enough subplots, such as those of Florimell and Marinell; Belphoebe and Timias; Sir Satyrane and the Squire of Dames; Malbecco, Hellenore, and Paridell; and Braggadochio and Trompart, are introduced so that Britomart herself is in danger of being forgotten. From the end of the flashback in which Merlin describes her descendants and she arms herself as a knight (Canto III) until her next significant action, the chase of the giant

Ollyphant leading to her aid of Sir Scudamore (Canto XI), the title heroine makes only two cameo appearances.

Surely a close analysis of a passage from *Euphues*, and an attempt to write Euphuistic prose or to imitate *Ada*, would have cured those tin ears, among other things, rendering that unintentional alliteration obvious. A careful attention to the *shape* of Lyly's sentences would have highlighted those morbid, dead-snake strings of prepositional phrases. To hear the *sound* of prose, a student must be schooled on the figures of sound. To see the *shape* of prose, he needs the figures of arrangement. If he then wants to put all these resources, all these delights, behind him and write prose as sparklingly clear as Baccarat crystal, let him. But if he is encouraged to write *only* this kind of scientific prose, he will *never write it at all*. White light is made of colors. It cannot be constituted out of nothing. Neither can a student's knowledge of scientific prose. The route to scientific clarity, the clarity The Books urge upon us with elephantine humorlessness, lies through the charming meadows of ornament. No other path leads to the stylistic awareness where good prose begins. Expository prose demands *Kunstprosa, prose poétique*.

We may now see what a disastrous influence linguistics promises to exert, indeed *is* exerting, on the teaching of writing. It departs from precisely the wrong premise. The linguist aims to get away from words altogether, embraces an algebraic symbolism and pretentious jargon that make him feel like a scientist and hence modern, but leave the verbal surface behind. Linguistics moves to the extreme right of our spectrum; it makes love to mathematics. We must go the other way—woo eloquence, not mathematics. We may come, joy of man's desiring, into a period of eloquence that demands the scientific attitude as a corrective. But we are not there yet. The rhetorical corrective is

what we need, and we need it badly. Only it can teach that
love of words for their own sake on which a healthy and
joyful American prose can be built, taught, and learned.
Only by seeing words, seeing prose style as a pleasure, can
we have any idea of how it might, or why it should, be a
duty.

4 The Delights of Jargon

Down with those who would refuse man the right to
professional speech.
                    Christopher Sykes, "What U-Future"

Definition, Samuel Johnson reminds us in Rambler 125,
stands outside the province of man. "There is scarcely any
species of writing, of which we can tell what is its essence,
and what are its constituents." Imagination always outstrips
our distinctions.

To attempt a definition of jargon threatens unusual
dangers. Jargon bears a high and highly indignant moral
charge, for one thing, and it pervades America, for another.
It usually means, Fowler says, "talk that is considered both
ugly sounding and hard to understand." Another usage
expert, Bergen Evans, reminds us that "jargon is a term of
contempt and must be used carefully." I use it more broadly
to mean styles serving special groups, interests, and activi-
ties. Its exclusively pejorative flavor—it is often hard to
understand because it wants to be, and by holding us at
arm's length adds offense to perplexity—blurs what it is,
how it works, and why it arose. No one can deny that
America in our time has produced the finest flowering of
specialist gobbledegook the planet has seen. Witness the
bureaucratic mumblespeak in chapter 2. American jargon
is such fun to contemplate, so full of pompous self-satisfac-
tion on the one hand and cynical, knowing, ritual mystification on the other that description hardly knows where to
begin. I choose, as in chapter 2, my own backyard, the
university. Consider this passage. It comes from a famous
study in sociological theory, *The Social System*, by a famous
sociologist, Talcott Parsons:

An element of a shared symbolic system which serves as a
criterion or standard for selection among the alternatives of

orientation which are intrinsically open in a situation may be called a value. . . . But from this motivational orientation aspect of the totality of action it is, in view of the role of symbolic systems, necessary to distinguish a "value-orientation" aspect. This aspect concerns, not the meaning of the expected state of affairs to the actor in terms of his gratification-deprivation balance but the content of the selective standards themselves. The concept of value-orientations in this sense is thus the logical device for formulating one central aspect of the articulation of cultural traditions into the action system.

It follows from the derivation of normative orientation and the role of values in action as stated above, that all values involve what may be called a social reference. . . . It is inherent in an action system that action is, to use one phrase, "normatively oriented." This follows, as was shown, from the concept of expectations and its place in action theory, especially in the "active" phase in which the actor pursues goals. Expectations then, in combination with the "double contingency" of the process of interaction as it has been called, create a crucially imperative problem of order. Two aspects of this problem of order may in turn be distinguished, order in the symbolic systems which make communication possible, and order in the mutuality of motivational orientation to the normative aspect of expectations, the 'Hobbesian' problem of order.

The problem of order, and thus of the nature of the integration of stable systems of social interaction, that is, of social structure, thus focuses on the integration of the motivation of actors with the normative cultural standards which integrate the action system, in our context interpersonally. These standards are, in the terms used in the preceding chapter, patterns of value-orientation, and as such are a particularly crucial part of the cultural tradition of the social system.

Typical Parsons, and not uncommon in the social sciences. Not everyone has Parsons's talent for this kind of prose, but most try. You wonder what it means? Fortunately, another sociologist of equal distinction though less orthodox profile, C. Wright Mills, has translated it into English (*The Sociological Imagination*, p. 27):

People often share standards and expect one another to stick to them. In so far as they do, their society may be orderly.

The social sciences increasingly provide the most popular majors in American universities. Students are being *taught* to write like this. Not, to be fair to most social scientists, taught directly. Not one in a thousand student papers in the social sciences is marked for style, up or down. But Parsons's kind of prose shines as an example. I came across a student in a composition class once who had actually been given a passage from Parsons on an examination. I asked her if she had understood it. What had she written as commentary? "Well, I couldn't figure out what it was about, you know, but, like, neither could the other kids, and I thought, like, they just wanted the same kind of bullshit back. So that's what I wrote. I got a B+." What kind of example had she been set? What does it exemplify?

First, it shows that the scientific ideal of clear, conceptual prose The Books dwell upon hasn't much application among working scientists. If you are a scientist, especially a social one, you had better *sound* scientific, the more scientific the better. Mills's clarity sounds so much less scientific than Parsons's sociologese. Mills's prose, clear, vigorous, sensible, the best plain prose of the scientific attitude, concentrates its energy on the subject. Parsons's prose aims to fix our gaze on the sociologist. What a wizard he must be to understand "motivational orientation aspect of the totality of action"— much less to pluck from such a nettle the rose, "value-orientation aspect." While the rest of us worry about "what other people will think," Parsons ponders that "it is inherent in an action system that action is, to use one phrase, 'normatively oriented.'" While we realize, after a couple of drinks, that society holds together because we mostly do what people expect us to, the social scientist perceives a deeper truth:

The problem of order, and thus of the nature of the integration of stable systems of social interaction, that is, of social structure, thus focuses on the integration of the motivation of actors with the normative cultural standards which integrate the action system, in our context interpersonally.

Imagine an undergraduate who reads nothing but this. He learns, knowingly or not, an important lesson—but in hypocrisy not sociology: never say what you mean simply. It sounds *too* simple. The lesson will stand him in good stead later, when he joins the bureaucracy of his choice. For prose like this is largely an exercise in the presentation of self. Parsons flatters Parsons. What he has to say about sociology can be said, as Mills points out, in twenty-five words or less. But he does not only flatter Parsons. He flatters all the sociologists who read him. What arcana they share! What bright chaps they must be to share them! Parsons's prose embarrasses us; coming from a teacher of the young, it should chill the blood. Only a strong hidden rhetoric could explain its appeal. Surely this rhetoric is the flattery, the ritual mystification that keeps the outsiders out and the insiders so pleased with themselves. We cannot condemn such prose as a failure. It has raised Parsons to wealth and honor; it has illuminated and refreshed innumerable social scientists of like mind. For them, it embodies clarity itself. It works, then, because it works upon sociologists not upon society. It gives them a flattering image of themselves and this, for good prose in the world outside composition class, remains the essential ingredient. To the bright student, young and breathless, it unveils a mystery. With energy, pluck, and luck, he too can join this group. Self-flattery and ritual mystification make effective recruiting posters.

Such a prose style does not stop at creating an image of the sociologist; it depicts a society. Read the passage again. Do you notice the strings of prepositional phrases? In the one sentence just singled out: *of* order, *of* the nature *of* the integration *of* stable systems *of* social interaction, *of* social structure, *on* the integration, *of* the motivation *of* actors *with* the normative cultural standards, *in* our context. The man writes entirely with prepositional phrases, all dependent on one another. Such sentences can have no shape or rhythm, they simply lurch forward from one preposition to the next. More important, such sentences consist almost entirely of *nouns*. The example just cited poses one main verb, "focuses," and one subordinate one, "integrate." For the rest, heaps of the Latinate "-ion" terminology that sets the tone of sociologese: interaction, integration, motivation, action. Verbs make things happen. To describe society with nouns rather than verbs implies the opposite of what (I think) Parsons wants to say. Here is a linguist on the noun-verb relationship (A. Meillet, *The Comparative Method in Historical Linguistics*, trans. G. B. Ford, Jr., p. 114):

We often observe this contrast between the absence of nominal inflection and the richness of the verbal inflection. This is due to the nature of the noun and the verb. The noun indicates an idea of permanent nature: a thing, a person, or a quality; the verb indicates a process. . . . For the very reason that it indicates a permanent notion, the noun has a sole form or at most a principal form from which the others are derived. On the other hand, the verb, which indicates a process, has personal forms and the expression of nuances which vary with languages, but can be numerous. The fact that the forms of the noun and verb obey divergent tendencies thus results from the nature of things.

"Meaning," then, in the Parsons passage, tells the student that society is a process, "style," that society stands still. Likely to be confused by the terminology, if he understands it he will become more so. Students learn the lessons such professional mystification teaches. If they are to join the system, they must learn to fool others—and more importantly to fool themselves—in precisely this way. Even as students, they must swim in it daily. Consider this memo circulated by the dean of students at a large state university:

During the 1969–1970 academic year, the [Frothingslosh U.] Student Services underwent a "participatory reconceptualiza-

tion." The participating groups included many individuals from
both senior and junior levels of staff. One of the many outcomes of
the reconceptualization was the recommendation that a Pilot
Decentralized Service Center be established for the 1970–1971
academic year. After some thought and discussion with various
staff members, we have decided to implement the recommendation.

The dean, like Parsons, teaches an important lesson, and
not only of prose.

Mystification for professional purposes is nothing new, of
course. An orthopedic surgeon I recently came to know had
just replaced a broken hip-joint with a plastic one. "The
prosthesis," he told me, "is in place." I was impressed. If he
had said, discarding the Greek derivative, "the ball-and-
socket is now glued in," he could not have charged $1500.
Jargons aim to define situations in flattering ways, and we
are, as often as not, included in the flattery. But, as in the
surgeon's case, the flattery seldom affects the surgery. It is,
like his secretary's white uniform, part of the flummery that
tries to justify exorbitant fees. In the academy, the flummery *becomes* the surgery. Students come to write like
Parsons, and to think like Parsons. Here is an example of a
first-rate student paper (it got an "A" and very kind words)
in linguistics.

The authors state that the learning of two languages from
childhood has favorable effects on the thinking process because,
"By constantly hearing the same things referred to by different
words from two languages the attention is drawn to the context
(essentials) instead of form." (p. 3) Although this argument is
based upon the idea that thought is dissociated from words, the
authors seem to infer that mere word association between
vocabularies of two languages encourages the bilingual child to
conceptualize. My opinion is that having two language vocabularies does not lead to conceptual thinking. Mental flexibility
arises from the bilingual's need to associate two languages'
different grammatical constructions and idiomatic expressions
and recognize that they refer to the same concepts.

A translation? "Learning two languages, the authors think, encourages a young child to think of concepts rather than words. I disagree. Grammatical and syntactical comparisons, much rather, stir him to think." The shapeless sentences, the flat, unemphatic assertion buried beneath a mound of "that's" and prepositional phrases—here, the student is taught, shines the true face of science. And she is writing about language and its relationship to concepts, *about* the scientific attitude toward prose!

It would be comforting to think of social scientists as the barbarians of the future and literary critics as priests attendant on the gemlike flame. Here is how one critic writes to the London *Times Literary Supplement* (May 28, 1971). America cannot be blamed here; the writer is a Cambridge don.

Sir,—it is disappointing to find Professor Fuller, in his lecture on science and poetry (May 14), rehearsing the traditionally grave arguments against the integrity of Shelley's imaginative procedures only to concede with facile judiciousness, that the old case must still stand. For thirty-five years later we might perhaps distinguish two components in Dr. Leavis's analysis: that in the sequence of overt or implied metaphor or simile the initial ground for comparison from which the figure rises often has less primacy in the direction of later development than the new areas of reference introduced by the figure; and that this induces confusion and exemplifies a damaging central weakness of mind.

Whatever interesting detail is unearthed about the hitherto less closely observed niceties of scientific reference in Shelley's vocabulary, the justice of the first component in this analysis cannot be disputed, and indeed it was a brilliantly shrewd piece of attentiveness to the uncongenial. What we may doubt is whether the second stage of the diagnosis *necessarily* follows from the first; and if not necessarily, then whether in a range of important particular cases it seems actually to describe our critical response. For we can by now surely see why, assuming on prior moral-epistemic grounds a *necessary* entailment, Dr. Leavis could hardly make dispassionate critical appraisal of the actualities.

Literary Parsonsese. The terms of art observe a higher tone
and do not so often break the jaw—"imaginative procedures, of acute judiciousness, sequence of overt or implied
metaphor or simile, less primacy in the direction of later
development, damaging central weakness of mind," and
later, "variable transfer of the criteria for imaginative
coherence, overlapping figurational transformation." But
the same aesthetic prevails. The critic walls out *hoi polloi,*
stages himself within as verbal magician, witch-doctor of
words. Of course he may actually think this way. "Literary
education," Northrop Frye reminds us (*The Well-Tempered
Critic*, p. 47), "should lead not merely to the admiration of
great literature, but to some possession of its power of
utterance." This is obviously not the case here, and is not
usually so, at least in America. Literary education seems to
make no difference at all to the utterance of most students
passing through it. In conversation, the student of literature
displays the same spastic drool of *likes, you knows,* and *wows*
that disfigure his mates in sociology and physics. His prose
crawls with the same painful spasms. No discipline is
exempt; only a few sin egregiously. Beyond the academy
walls, the same flapdoodle is retailed, the retailers being less
culpable since, though the young are betrayed, the be-
trayers do not masquerade as teachers.

We are, clearly enough, deep into the moral attitude
toward prose. Confronted with Parsons's prose, it is hard to
keep perspective. For students, it must be hard to keep a
balanced mind. Imagine one hour spent reading Shakespeare's sonnets, and the next with this:

When the integrated part of the mind has been distorted in a
bygone period by an unusual splitting off of those aspects of
established functions which precipitated experiences of over-
whelming disorganization or unpleasure as they were being
increasingly utilized by normally emerging instinctual drive
representatives, then the split-off portion can be regarded as a
surviving representative of instinctual operations responsible for

the formation or the maintenance of phase-specific mental organization. [Theodore Lipin, "Sensory Irruptions and Mental Organization," *Journal of the American Psychoanalytic Association*, vol. 17, no. 4]

No wonder students begin to feel schizzy. Change classes, change worlds. Inevitable—and enjoyable—as the moral attitude is toward mumblespeak, such an attitude offers neither remedy nor pedagogy. Plenty of people deplore-with-grave-concern the jargon scene. But moralizing offers no way out. It will not reform professors who fool their students with mumbo-jumbo. It will not keep bureaucrats from playing variations on "That's not my department." It will not commit to truth a politician aiming to commit himself to nothing, or prohibit university presidents from marketing exuberant inanities. Jargons, like other styles, respond to situations. To prevent them, we must change the situation. Freshman Composition will not bring such a change. Moralizing composition teachers pray that if you get the cant out of someone's prose, you will get the cant out of his mind. No evidence supports such optimism. Once again, what to do? Give up? No. Give in.

I was once sitting in a faculty meeting listening to the mumblespeak fall like gentle rain. A new colleague, fresh to the scene and, worse, an Englishman, whispered in my ear, "My God, is it always like this?" It is. But I surprised myself. I was not offended by the mumblespeak, I was enjoying it. I was simultaneously translating it into English, trying—purely as one Anthropoid Input, of course—to guess between whose shoulder blades the next "ongoing reappraisal" would strike, praying for an "incremental adjustment" (raise in salary), keeping a five-count—a long-standing habit—of "the fact that" and "like you know." Nonsense turned into game. Such an epiphany did not fail of pedagogical implication. I could not metamor-phose the speaker into a sensible man, supply a sense of

humor, inject a liberal education. No more can a student
cut off the daily flow of jargon he drowns in. But he can be
taught to recognize it, see through it, even laugh at it. If you
cannot reform nonsense you may learn to banquet off it. For
this, the moral attitude helps.

First, you must translate jargon into English. But the job
only begins here. You must also understand what situation
a jargon responds to, how it works. Learn the languages.
The desired result seems that yielded by foreign language
study—reflection on the nature of language itself, the
limitations it imposes on our knowing and expressing. More
than this, another language pleases in itself. Even a
mumblespeak supplies a new conceptual world, complete
with intriguing bafflements and charming mysteries. To
survive in a world of mumblespeaks, use the comparative
method, become a connoisseur. This is no unhopeful thing,
as we shall see. The connoisseur strategy is an old one but
promises to flourish again now. Starting with an old and
famous example of such stylistic debunking, we move to
several modern instances.

The oldest jargon, if poetry really did precede prose
historically, is the language of poetry, "poetic diction." Not
usually ugly, grasping no *parti-pris* advantage, it exists—as
all jargons finally do—for pleasure. Alexander Pope, in
attacking the poetic diction of his day in *Peri Bathous*,
employed the exemplary strategy for dealing with jargon.
His title parodies Longinus's treatise on sublimity and its
high style, "*Peri Hupsous*: The Art of Soaring in Poetry," in
"The Art of Sinking in Poetry." His essay creates its stylistic
comedy by applying a scientific attitude to an opaque style.
Such should be the fundamental strategy for dealing with
jargon. Not moral reproach but translation and imitation
best create comic awareness. Here are some of Pope's
translations:

> Who knocks at the Door?
> For whom thus rudely pleads my loud-tongued gate,

That he may enter? . . .
     See who is there?
Advance the fringed curtains of thy eyes,
And tell me who comes yonder . . .
     Shut the Door.
The wooden guardian of our privacy
Quick on its axle turn . . .
     Bring my Clothes.
Bring me what Nature, tailor to the *Bear*,
To *Man* himself denied: She gave me *Cold*,
But would not give me Clothes . . .
     Light the Fire.
Bring forth some remnant of *Promethean* theft,
Quick to expand th'inclement air congealed
By *Boreas'* rude breath . . .
     Snuff the candle.
Yon Luminary amputation needs,
Thus shall you save its half-extinguished life.
     Open the Letter.
Wax! render up thy trust . . . .
   Uncork the Bottle, and chip the Bread.
Apply thine engine to the spongy door,
Set *Bacchus* from his glassy prison free,
And strip white *Ceres* of her nut-brown coat.

Jargon's wellspring stands exposed—to flatter ordinary reality. Pope, no more than C. Wright Mills, pauses over this flattery. Both see jargon only as the last stage in stylistic disintegration. True enough, in Pope's day and ours. But might not our jargon explosion be an encouraging sign, too?

Moralistic critics of jargon see it as corrupting, maliciously or mindlessly, a preexistent scientific clarity. They consider it what the Latin rhetoricians called a *color,* a strategy to present your case in its most favorable light. We began this chapter by varying such a theme. But even sociologese deserves a kindlier gaze. In the first place, necessity often demands a terminology. Unless continually redefined, it must seem arcane. However stupifying its

sound to an outsider, familiarity renders it agreeable to
cognoscenti. Familiarity creates clarity. But beyond need
and rhetorical or psychological advantage lies the fun of a
special language. Amidst the moral disapproval of jargon as
debasing the means of conscious life, no one has noticed
that jargons are fun—and not simply to their connoisseur
but to their user, self-conscious or not.

People seldom content themselves with plain utterance
even in daily life. It gets boring. They invent tautological
and periphrastic equivalents to relieve the tedium. They
prefer the metaphorical, the indirect expression to the
straightforward, literal one. They are not trying to be
literary. Metaphors are just more fun. With stylized
phrases, all kinds of attitudes, feelings, in-jokes come to
life—a whole range of expressivity that scientific prose
excludes. Here the cliché was begotten—for pleasure—by
Variety on Familiarity. Frank Sullivan illustrated this
surprising paternity in an immortal *New Yorker* piece
(August 31, 1935) called "The Cliché Expert Takes the
Stand."

Q—Mr. Arbuthnot, you are an expert in the use of the cliché, are
      you not?

A—Yes, sir, I am a certified public cliché expert.

Q—In that case would you be good enough to answer a few
      questions on the use and application of the cliché in ordinary
      speech and writing?

A—I should be only too glad to do so.

Q—Thank you. Now, just for the record—you live in New York?

A—I like to visit New York but I wouldn't live here if you gave
      me the place.

Q—Then where do you live?

A—Any old place I hang my hat is home sweet home to me.

Q—What is your age?

A—I am fat, fair, and forty.

Q—And your occupation?

A—Well, after burning the midnight oil at an institution of

higher learning, I was for a time a tiller of the soil. Then I went down to the sea in ships for a while, and later, at various times, I have been a guardian of the law, a gentleman of the Fourth Estate, a poet at heart, a bon vivant and raconteur, a prominent clubman and man about town, an eminent——

Q—Just what is your occupation at the moment, Mr. Arbuthnot?

A—At the moment I am an unidentified man of about forty, shabbily clad.

Q—Now then, Mr. Arbuthnot, what kind of existence do you, as a cliché expert, lead?

A—A precarious existence.

Q—And what do you do to a precarious existence?

A—I eke it out.

Q—Have you ever been in a kettle of fish?

A—Oh, yes.

Q—What kind?

A—A pretty kettle of fish.

Q—How do you cliché experts reveal yourselves, Mr. Arbuthnot?

A—In our true colors, of course.

Q—And you expect to live to . . .

A—A ripe old age.

Q—What do you shuffle off?

A—This mortal coil.

Q—What do you thank?

A—My lucky stars.

Q—What kind of retreats do you like?

A—Hasty retreats.

Q—What do you do to hasty retreats?

A—I beat them.

Clichés are petrified metaphors. The moralist stresses the petrified, berates stale language and, if a critic, numbers the blessings of poetry. Poetry, by putting language under pressure in new verbal environments, creates it anew, refreshes it, invents new metaphors or, like Sullivan, galvanizes the clichés with irony. Stress the *metaphor* and we see jargon begin. Clichés work paradoxically, as a generally shared specialist language (special to situations, not speakers). They develop from the pleasures men take in language. They live in the play impulse, the play attitude toward style. They are often ironized, "super-enclichéd," before the essayist embraces them. So we say not "Oh, I can make myself comfortable anywhere" but "Any old place I hang my hat is home sweet home to me." "Home sweet home" provides a nicely domestic cliché to bounce your freedom against, and hanging your hat is a human gesture, not a concept like "making yourself at home." We've all done it—or did it when people wore hats—and can enhance it with a whole vocabulary of gestures and attitudes. In Stendhal's definition, it has style, action, plus circumambient attitudes.

If, at forty, we say "I am forty, slightly overweight, but quite contented with life, thank you very much," we are clear, as The Books demand, but miss the pleasures of alliteration. If we have studied at a university, then farmed, then sailed the seas, we may say so thus. But such a statement, to be applauded for its clarity, its avoidance (how The Books dwell on this) of cliché, has no past. If we burn the midnight oil, we tread in the footsteps of Horace; if we till the soil, our tilth has biblical precedent. And being in an "uncomfortable situation" can hardly compare to a warm and companionable kettle of fish. When it is all over, who would simply die when he could, with comfy panâche, kick the bucket? Such expressions are fun to tease because they were fun to begin with. They illustrate man's natural flight from plain statement, from the scientific to the play attitude toward style.

Jargon is like rhetoric. It always describes what the *other* guy does. We argue, he indulges in specious rhetoric. We make ourselves clear, he speaks jargon. All of us languish in the grip of the scientific attitude. Unwilling to grant the other fellow his pleasures, we cannot forego our own. We might see more clearly would we acknowledge—and develop—our common pleasure in words. As Kenneth Burke wrote, on eloquence (*Counter-Statement*, p. 167):

The primary purpose of eloquence is not to enable us to live our lives on paper—it is to convert life into its most thorough verbal equivalent. The categorical appeal of literature resides in a liking for verbalization as such, just as the categorical appeal of music resides in a liking for musical sounds as such.

We feel an irrepressible urge to render our experience literary, metaphorical, scaled to and intimately involved with man. We want to render it, not clear and scientific, but rich, human, full of indirection. Burke discusses the pressure within a literary work to intricate itself "until in all its smallest details the work bristles with disclosures, contrasts, restatements with a difference, ellipses, images, aphorism, volume, sound-values, in short all that complex wealth of minutiae which in their line-for-line aspect we call style" (*Counter-Statement*, p. 38).

We must learn to think of jargon thus kindly, as an effort toward style. Our current tidal wave of it may well be created by our national effort to be clear, to write prose exclusively under the scientific rubric. The need for style thus rushes in through the back door of jargon, disheveled and dirty, unprepossessing, but testifying to an ancient hunger. Another kind of book might pause to anatomize American bad taste, explaining it, in the same way, as the play attitude's response to an overstressed scientific attitude toward style. For prose, the lesson stands plain. If you aim only at a scientific style, you will end up with a bad style, with ugly jargon and comic debunking as the only corrective. The wave of jargon, testifying to an unsatisfied love of words, a starved play attitude toward style, may presage a countercycle.

Jargon, then, can gesture toward belonging, toward social solidarity. It can present a version of self. It can play. Added up, these constitute something like the opaque style

discussed earlier. Jargon yields that stylistic self-consciousness shared by reader and writer which renders style a
subject, an acknowledged way of looking at the world.
Jargon always moves in this direction; however *lumpen*, it
approaches the lightness of play. Ample illustration of this
movement has been provided in the last few years by
frequent spoofs of the computerized and militarized govern-
ment jargon called bureaucratese. One of them ("New Peak
for Newspeak," *Newsweek*, May 6, 1968) begins:

After a recent Vietnam bombing mission, a B-52 pilot summed
up the day's work as an "effective ordnance delivery" (translation: target demolished). When George Romney abruptly exited
from the Presidential race, his New Hampshire campaign man-
ager explained that the candidate believed he lacked "a positive
reference input" (translation: a good image). In its January letter
to shareholders, Litton Industries attributed declining stock
profits to "volume variances from plan" (translation: strikes).

Once confined to Mad Ave and Foggy Bottom, Euphemisms,
circumlocutions, jargon and other high-flown forms of linguistic
obfuscation have now become as pervasive as pollution. From San
Antonio (where the sidewalks at HemisFair are called "people
expressways") to New York City (where a garage mechanic
advertises himself as an "automotive internist"), the word is out
that anything goes verbalizationwise.

Physicians are starting to call pep pills "activity boosters." A
Milwaukee brokerage house recently touted a certain stock
because it had "a small downside risk with a worthwhile upside
potential." Preschoolers are now enrolled in "early learning
centers," where they orbit between their "pupil stations" (desks)
and the "instructional materials resource center" (library).

This election year will witness its share of confrontations,
accommodations and reconciliations. "You have to watch the
words that are being tossed around these days," observes Sen.
Eugene McCarthy. "You never know what you're getting into."
Even superliterates like William Buckley Jr. occasionally contribute to the mess. During a TV appearance, Buckley closed a
176-word answer to a question by observing ". . . and this

seemed to me a centrifugalization, a social centrifugalization which would cut the whole energy circuit of civilizations."

Sugar Coating: Much of the word pollution results from a tropistic reaction to a disagreeable truth. As the problems of Vietnam, race and poverty grow more complex and pressing, the need for sugar-coated palliatives grows more insistent. Vietnam has popularized "gradualism," "infrastructure" and "defoliation," while prompting one State Department official to suggest that U.S. bombing pressure on the enemy "should be mainly violins, but with periodic touches of brass" (more selective than massive). Such gibberish, observes Yale professor of psychiatry Robert Lifton, "helps psychically numb people to what's happening on the other side of the weapon."

Even from behind so moral, so grisly a context, the spirit of play peeps out. It does so still more in the game, "How to win at wordsmanship," appended to the article:

After years of hacking through etymological thickets at the U.S. Public Health Service, a 63-year-old official named Philip Broughton hit upon a sure-fire method for converting frustration into fulfillment (jargonwise). Euphemistically called the Systematic Buzz Phrase Projector, Broughton's system employs a lexicon of 30 carefully chosen "buzzwords":

Column 1	Column 2	Column 3
0. integrated	0. management	0. options
1. total	1. organizational	1. flexibility
2. systematized	2. monitored	2. capability
3. parallel	3. reciprocal	3. mobility
4. functional	4. digital	4. programming
5. responsive	5. logistical	5. concept
6. optional	6. transitional	6. time-phase
7. synchronized	7. incremental	7. projection
8. compatible	8. third-generation	8. hardware
9. balanced	9. policy	9. contingency

The procedure is simple. Think of any three-digit number, then select the corresponding buzzword from each column. For instance, number 257 produces "systematized logistical projection," a phrase that can be dropped into virtually any report with that ring of decisive, knowledgeable authority. "No one will have the remotest idea of what you're talking about," says Broughton, "but the important thing is that they're not about to admit it."

Here we jump wholly into the game sphere, into that childlike state that puts words together for the fun of it, freeing them from the need to make sense. Notice how all the words in the game are scientific? Scientific prose, pushed as far as it will go, turns into a game. The ends of the spectrum meet to make it a circle.

As relief from the straight society's jargon we might, like many others, lust after hippie delights. The hip world has deliberately cultivated a second language. Modeled originally on the argot of the black ghetto, it has been taken over for just the reasons that all jargons are devised, to protect a group, enhance its sense of identity, express the concepts peculiar to it, and to have fun. Several glossaries of hip talk have been compiled to guide the straights. Here is a brief excerpt from Lewis Yablonsky's brilliant and humane study, *The Hippie Trip*:

> Bag: a personal area of involvement or interest, as in "That's his bag"
>
> Behind-it: sincerely committed to a particular subject or action
>
> Bread: money
>
> Bug: bother, annoy
>
> Bummer: an emotionally unpleasant or upsetting experience; also, a negative drug reaction, as an LSD "bummer"
>
> Burned: cheated
>
> Busted: arrested
>
> Clark Kent hippies: part-timers who live mainly in straight society; weekend hippies
>
> Cop-out: to confess, or to compromise one's position or beliefs
>
> Cool: to be tuned-in, into things
>
> Cut out: leave
>
> Dig: enjoy, appreciate, understand
>
> Far out: unusual, extraordinary; bizarre or avant-garde

Flash-on: to think about; become intensely aware of or remember

Freak-out: to lose control, to have bizarre patterns of thought or behavior. Often occurring under the influence of a drug

Grass: marijuana

Groove: to "swing," to enjoy, to be "with it"

Hassle: an annoyance or conflict situation

Head: a frequent user of psychedelic drugs, as in acid-head or pot-head

Heat: police

Hip: to be "in," "with it," emotionally wise, in the know

Joint: marijuana cigarette

Man (the): police; or drug dealer

Out front: open; honest; or the preface to a statement

Out of sight: so good that words fail to describe it

Rap: to talk; or present one's particular point of view

Roach: butt of a marijuana cigarette

Spade: a Negro. Used in a nondiscriminatory way

Split: to leave

Square: a person or thing, not tuned-in or in the know

Stoned: very high on drugs

Teenybopper: a teenage "plastic" hippie

Turn-on: to use a drug; to get into the new scene

Up-tight: overly anxious or nervous

This jargon, though not without its nightmares, its bad-tripping speed freaks who never come down, seems a charm and a delight compared to bureaucratic mumblespeak. The reasons are not far to seek. It does not try to be scientific. Like the movement it enshrines, it grounds itself in feelings, not concepts, in metaphor, in the play attitude, not the scientific or moral ones. The glossary cited is pure metaphor, folk poetry, cliché being born. (The terms may solidify into ironic cliché in the hip world, as they have already done outside. "Right on!" for the straights now signifies a heavily ironic approval.)

A comparison of sociological or governmental mumblespeak with hip talk carries us deep into the social problems that bedevil us. Mumblespeak aims above all to sound impersonal, conceptual. No people live in it. It is not *written*, it precipitates out of a committee: "It was decided that," "a significant implementation was effected." It gets as far away as it can from people and their unashamedly metaphorical attempts to cope with the world. It masquerades as inevitable historical process. It waddles concept-heavy, obese with nouns. Notice, in the hip glossary, how many verbs there are? How many expressions—*high, up front, behind it*—imply movement or physical location? How close the terms stay to basic realities of human life? The bureaucrat speaks of the "appropriate regulatory authorities," the hippie of "the heat."

Let us try a more extended example. Here are two discussions of sex. The first, an article entitled "Voluntary Control of Eroticism" (Donald E. Henson and H. B. Rubin, *Journal of Applied Behavior Analysis*, vol. 4, no. 1) investigates, you see at last, whether men watching dirty movies can voluntarily avoid having an erection.

Laws and Rubin (1961) reported that penile erection, an autonomic visceral response (Kelly, 1961) that is generally considered involuntary . . . could be voluntarily controlled by normal male subjects. Their subjects were able both to produce erections in the absence of erotic stimuli and inhibit erections in the presence of effective erotic stimulation. Each subject reported that tumescence was achieved by "fantasizing" about erotic events, and that inhibition was accomplished by producing competing stimuli, i.e., concentrating on asexual stimuli. . . .

Since the attending indicator of the Laws and Rubin study (1969) ensured attendance only to the display area of the erotic stimulation, the contention can be made that their subjects were not attending to the content of the stimuli when voluntary inhibition occurred. However, if penile inhibition is possible when attendance to the content of erotic stimulation is guaranteed, then it must be assumed that the automatic visceral response of penile erection can be at least partially modified by voluntary controls.

Subjects

Eight adult males (age 21 to 30 yrs.) volunteered to serve as subjects. Two (S-1 and S-2) were employees of Anna State Hospital, had participated in an earlier study . . . , and received no remuneration. Three subjects (S-3, S-4, and S-5) were experimentally naive, were students at Southern Illinois University, and were remunerated for their transportation and time at the rate of $2.50 per hour.

The remaining three subjects did not complete the study, two because during their baseline test session, sample stimulus films were ineffective in eliciting full penile erection, and the third because he attempted to control his penile erection by manipulating his penis. All subjects were fully informed of the nature of the experiment.

For contrast, here is an East Village hippie describing the sexual customs of that scene (*The Hippie Trip*, pp. 121–22):

There are girls around here that hit on guys—two or three different guys a day sometimes. It's much freer here. When you are in a group and you and a girl want to ball and there are some guys with you and you want to get rid of them you don't try to explain to them. Like if you were at school or something, you know, like "Would you do us a favor—go out and get us some ice cream or something?" But here you just say, "Now look, I'm going in that room and that room is the 'ball room,' you know, I'm going to do 'my thing,' excuse me for a while." The way it is back home, everybody knows that girls are getting screwed and that guys are having a good time. I mean, everybody knows that. Ninety-five percent of the girls in the school I went to were not virgins. Everybody knows that. But the first time that the fact comes out that a girl has been screwed in school, automatically she becomes a whore. Here it is different. Like I mean, back home there are lots of girls getting screwed in school, you know, and everybody secretively knows it. But the first time somebody comes along and says, "Hey, Mary got screwed last night," everybody starts on the big thing that Mary is a whore. Now here, like Mary got screwed last night and she went and did it, well, gee whiz, good enough—wow, I mean what's it to me? I mean, wow, that's the way it is here.

No point in talking about which style is *better*. Both make us laugh. The first, preoccupied with a subject that creates ribaldry almost spontaneously, bends over backwards to keep a scientific straight face. In fact, the authors create delightful stylistic comedy. Content and style stand so far apart in this prose that the ordinary reader (though not, I suppose, the social scientist) responds, as the experiment progresses from stage to humorless stage, with burgeoning laughter. If the authors had written the experiment up in ordinary prose, of course, no journal would have published it—no status trip. Plain language would not have made the prose less scientific, but it would have *seemed* so. Hence the jargon.

The hippie's explanation of ballroom etiquette, by contrast, stays close to the surface of experience. Not scientific —a social scientist would write "fornicatorium" not "ballroom"—it is direct, immediate, intensely metaphorical. Compared to the "Voluntary Control of Eroticism" it lives, that's all. It would be a mistake to call it a plain style. It gets down to facts through *metaphor*. For example, take that most delicate of all problems, words for the sex act. English, let alone American, has no word that simply expresses sexual intercourse without implying an attitude. *Screw* is lewd, *make love* euphemistic, *fornicate* biblical, *copulate* clinical, *fuck* vulgar. So one is devised: *to ball*. New expression for a new attitude toward sex. Could sociologists capable of the mumblespeak we have just read ever develop the stylistic awareness needed to see the changing social attitudes behind "you and a girl want to ball"?

The hip jargon here quoted is, like all hippie jargon, hip *talk*. You cannot imagine anyone ever *speaking or reading aloud*, "Voluntary Control of Eroticism." It is unreadable. Consequently, it possesses no rhythm, no life. It is otherwise with young Brian (age eighteen) chronicling hippie sex. Read the passage aloud. You catch intonation and stress immediately. Part of American tone-deafness has been an addiction to a pitchless monotone. Change in pitch is natural to hippie talk, just as it is to black speech. Change in pitch, in fact, often signifies change in meaning. As in any limited vocabulary (and hip-talk has a very limited vocabulary) one word serves many uses. Listen to a dozen *out of sight*'s or *too much*'s. You'll notice that pitch makes meaning. This creates a speech more agreeable to listen to.

Northrop Frye calls such rhythm "associative" and thinks the habits of hippie speech are corruptions of it. Endless interruptions of *like* and *you know*, utterance begun and left hanging, betoken an ego running free, out of control. He is surely right, and yet, in the passage we have, don't we see, too, a hunger for style, for a style closer to experience than the scientific attitude allows? Like everything else in the hippie world, hip jargon adumbrates problems in the straight world. What surfaces here is dissatisfaction with the remote inhumanity, the impersonality of journalistic reporting, of mumblespeak, of the preposterous drivel that politicians talk. An example of this last is President Nixon's First Inaugural Address:

I ask you to share with me today the majesty of this moment. In the orderly transfer of power, we celebrate the unity that keeps us free.

Each moment in history is a fleeting time, precious and unique. But some stand out as moments of beginning, in which courses are set that shape decades or centuries.

This can be such a moment.

Forces now are converging that make possible, for the first time, the hope that many of man's deepest aspirations can at last be realized. The spiraling pace of change allows us to contemplate, within our own lifetime, advances that once would have taken centuries.

In throwing wide the horizons of space, we have discovered new horizons on earth.

For the first time, because the people of the world want peace, and the leaders of the world are afraid of war, the times are on the side of peace.

Eight years from now America will celebrate its 200th anniversary as a nation. Within the lifetime of most people now living, mankind will celebrate that great new year which comes only once in a thousand years—the beginning of the third millennium.

What kind of a nation we will be, what kind of a world we will live in, whether we shape the future in the image of our hopes, is ours to determine by our actions and our choices.

Prose like this renders suspect all words except the fundamental ones. So you use those over and over. At least they don't share the taint of patent hypocrisy that public prose like this drags in from "the plastic world" (another hip metaphor).

Hip talk succeeds in re-creating their world for people who don't know it firsthand. We should not, however, sentimentalize it. The stock responses, the simplistic opinions, the persistent, pure mindlessness of the hippie trip, come through loud and clear. But their language does shine with life and humor. Mumblespeak, equally expressive of its milieu, offers neither. Both jargons "work." A comparison must choose, not styles but worlds, life-styles, ways to live.

For diversion, imagine young Brian in Freshman Composition. Most composition teachers, in fact, do not need to imagine him at all. He'll be—or probably not be—in class tomorrow. The topic for the day: "What I Did Last Summer." So Brian tells all. It comes out as above. What to do? The Books, of course, all have a section on jargon. It's probably called, in the schematic end-paper *index errorum*, "Jarg." The Books are not having any Jargs. If you are Walter Scott and a Scot and writing about Scottish conversation, maybe you can try Jarg, if you call it "Dial." Otherwise not. The Books can't cope with Brian's style because Brian's *attitude* toward style does not figure in their stylistic universe. Try to normalize it according to the scientific attitude, and it vanishes. Yet it is not fiction. It is actual conversation, transcribed from a tape (and surely this is how some students now write their "papers"). It is genuinely comic not, like "Voluntary Eroticism," unintentionally so. In any sense in which the phrase means anything, it "has style." Yet it is clearly a jargon and contaminated with the worst associative rhythms, the *like* and *you know* speech disease.

"Scientific language," a famous Harvard linguist tells us, "tends to surmount language, so as to overcome the vernacular, and to become universal" (Joshua Whatmough, *Language*, p. 102). Hip talk constitutes a plea for the vernacular and the pleasures of jargon at the same time. It is not without pedagogical implications. Any scheme of prose style that does not have room for it and styles like it—and not simply room to condemn—should be scrapped. Stylistic experience constitutes a full continuum. It is never turned off. We should be able to make sense of—ideally, to relish—any style, especially those which surround us. A scheme that can describe Sir Thomas Browne's "Urn-Burial" but not Brian's disquisition on balling is worse than useless. Worse, because it reinforces the worst of American errors, the delusion that style is only for poetry, for the classroom, not for—and part of—everyday life.

The obvious therapy is not only to normalize jargons but to imitate them, parody them, and translate them one into another. America possesses no central normative prose style considered that of an educated man, no BBC English. We haven't the social structure a normative style emerges from and is built upon. Americans are born eclectics, in prose as in every other kind of style. Why not make the most of it?

5 Poetic Prose

εὖ νυν τόδ᾽ ἐξεπίστασο, ὡς ἐν τοῖσι ὠσὶ
τῶν ἀνθρώπων οἰκέει ὁ θυμός

[The way to a man's heart is through his ears.]

Xerxes, in Herodotus 7.39

Most theorists agree with The Books that, whatever a prose style should be, it cannot be "poetic." By this are meant many things. Prose cannot let its style show, in other words, cannot employ an opaque style. It cannot use the obvious rhetorical figures of sound and arrangement. It cannot allow style to become subject. It must express its subject but not change it by the mode of expression. A poem exists for its own sake, it serves itself. Prose must never do this. As Sir Herbert Read epigrammatizes it (*English Prose Style*, p. ix), "Poetry is creative expression: prose is constructive expression." The two modes of expression reflect two fundamentally different ways of thinking: "Poetry is the expression of one form of mental activity. Prose is the expression of another form." Prose is loyal to concepts, poetry to image, to itself. In a poem, writes the famous linguist Roman Jakobson, the coding interests us more than the message.

Reversing that definition fits it nicely to prose—in prose, the message predominates. Prose belongs to the intellect, poetry to the emotions. As Murry (*The Problem of Style*, pp. 60–61) writes:

The specific virtue of prose is that it is judicial; and that is a virtue that poetry cannot have: if it has, it is not poetry, but prose in metre. Where the appeal is to the judgment, there the vehicle is prose: if the appeal is made with absolute economy, so that the movement is swift and certain to the conclusion, then it will give an aesthetic pleasure over and above its convincing force.

Metrical form does not separate prose from poetry, nor does

density of metaphorical language. The nature of the appeal, the part of man's nature addressed, is what governs. An overplus of energy and effect, the job very well done, supplies a bonus that is aesthetic but fortuitous. Loyalty must incline to concept and conceptual intelligence. Murry makes the distinction historical: "Why was prose developed, if not to afford expression to a content which suffered by being thrust into metrical form?" Such a distinction turns on our three attitudes toward style—scientific, moral, and playful. Once again, the playful, or aesthetic, ingredient must linger outside the walls. This is poetry's domain. Information and the moral censor that verifies it must animate prose.

The trouble with this definition is the worst trouble a definition can have. It ignores most of the definiendum, the thing defined. It defines, in its purity, only mathematics. And it confuses students of literature, beginning and professional, to the last degree. Description rather than definition seems in order. We may view any utterance with any one of the three attitudes, or any combination of them. We may read poetry for the story and thus invoke the scientific attitude by demanding information. An experienced bureaucrat may search a conference report for minute hints of attitude, less for what was said than for how old Charley said it, whether old Charley's head would roll and his replace it. The prose may be vintage mumblespeak, but he, alert to symbol and metaphor, will read it as poetry, for attitude and feeling.

Nobody can—and nobody should—make rules about what prose can do. It can do anything language can do. To say that if it does certain things it becomes poetry confuses to no purpose. Reference to the non-invidious stylistic spectrum makes more sense and works as well for poetry as for prose. To what extent is style an issue? How self-conscious is the reader-writer relationship? Such a location, easy and informative, spares us the agonies of redefinition required to distinguish fictional prose from nonfictional. The traditional scientific and moral definitions of prose obviously do not apply to fictional prose, so it must be poetry. And what about a prose that is fictional but reportorial? Or, as in Truman Capote's *In Cold Blood*, factual but very fictional too (a "faction," as they are now called)? The whole definition collapses into such conundrums. Fictional prose is simply prose where the play attitude, the formal expectation, figures as strongly as the scientific expectation, sometimes more so. "Poetic" prose— fictional or not—simply moves further over on the spectrum.

No fundamental difference separates fictional from nonfictional prose, just as none divides prose and poetry. Any attitude, or combination of attitudes, may inform either pair, although perhaps the scientific attitude most often informs nonfictional prose. But to say so, you must do two things seldom done: read the prose carefully with the play attitude to see how the form works, and survey all the prose that has ever been written. The statement demands, and lends itself, at least theoretically, to quantitative proof. When critics say prose most often conveys information, they mean they usually read prose for information, and of course they find what they seek. Agree that the scientific attitude should prevail, and so it will. The pontificating task-force master quoted earlier suffers acutely from the scientific attitude. He wears it like blinders. He cannot see how his utterance betrays his character. He sees information; the audience sees a donkey. The only therapy can be the active presence of all three attitudes.

Can no distinction, then, be made between prose and poetry? The only one stares us in the face—the typographical one. And this amounts, finally, to signifying an appropriate attitude toward the reader. You arrange words in a certain linear pattern. This tells the reader the formal attitude is appropriate. To find to what degree it fits, one must read on. But the point is clear: poetic typography invites an attitude toward style. Few critics now contend that such an arrangement demands a certain subject, that poetry must treat a poetic subject. But most students of prose still insist that absence of this typographical arrangement *does* bring with it a certain subject matter. Poetry does not have an intrinsically poetic subject, but prose must have an intrinsically prosaic one. This is mindless.

To experiment, I look up at the bookshelves above my desk for the most "prosaic" book there. Dictionaries excluded, the choice falls on Goodwin and Gulick's *Greek Grammar*. In the *sortes virgilianae* manner, I open it by chance to p. 312, a discussion of indirect discourse:

In
   direct Dis   course or Or
   ati-   o Ob
   liqua
A direct quotation
      or question gives   the exact words
of the original speaker
     or writer.
In an in direct quotation
         or question   the original words
   conform   to the
   construction of the
   sentence   in which   they are
   quoted.

What's happening? The typography forces the play attitude on a piece of authentically scientific prose. The similarity in shape of "Indirect" and "A direct" is enforced by putting them on different lines. The *o* vowel sounds (-or-Or o-Ob) are pointed to by typographical clustering; so, too, *-ati-* and *-liqua-* for *a* sounds. "Quotation" and "question" begin with the same letter, and similarly, and contain nearly the same number of syllables. So they go together. *In-an-in* makes a nice sound play and so that gets isolated. And we want to pile up the nouns that matter, those that form the passage's center. So we do that typographically too, stacking them up. And *the exact words* and *the original words* earn a separate grouping by beginning and ending alike and by admitting antithetical comparison from the sense of the passage.

We might write a good deal of prosaic poetry as prose, unmask it as "just verse," deny the versifier a privilege we accord the poet, to invoke an attitude by typographical convention. Poeticizing poor Goodwin and Gulick reveals the "poetic" attitude we can bring to the driest stuff if we choose, but it does not show so fully as it might how even the best poet, the most practiced reader, depends on typography. Anyone who has tried to read a Greek manuscript written without word or line divisions will know how profoundly disoriented the modern reader feels, bereft of typographical convention.

We may get some idea of this by simply writing out a familiar sonnet in prose. I shall not indent it here, since that itself lends a kind of emphasis. "Margaret, are you grieving over golden grove unleaving? Leaves, like the things of man, you, with your fresh thoughts care for, can you? Ah! As the heart grows older, it will come to such sights colder, by and by, nor spare a sigh, though worlds of wanwood leafmeal lie. And yet you will weep, and know why. Now, no matter, child, the name. Sorrow's springs are the same. Nor mouth had, no, nor mind expressed, what heart heard of, ghost guessed. It is the blight man was born for. It is Margaret you mourn for." I've tinkered with the punctuation a bit and omitted the accent marks Hopkins supplies. What's left is no more "Spring and Fall" than what comes to Southern California.

I wanted this example, like the first, to be extreme. It shows up our attitudes so much better. Hopkins's exquisite sonnet resists prosing as much as any poem can. Yet how it sings in verse:

> Márgarét, are you grieving
> Over Goldengrove unleaving?

Léaves, like the things of man, you
With your fresh thoughts care for, can you?
Áh! ás the heart grows older
It will come to such sights colder
By and by, nor spare a sigh
Though worlds of wanwood leafmeal lie,
And yet you wíll weep and know why.
Now no matter, child the name:
Sórrow's spríngs áre the same.
Nor mouth had, no nor mind, expressed
What heart heard of, ghost guessed:
It ís the blight man was born for,
It is Margaret you mourn for.

"Spring and Fall" enforces differences between prose and
verse usually considered essential, meter and rhyme. Prose
cannot be preponderantly regular in its rhythm, cannot
have, though it may occasionally use, meter. Nor can it
rhyme with frequency or pattern. The distinction is a clear
one, but what good is it? To say that any written utterance
which uses meter and rhyme past an arbitrarily decided
point must be called poetry, simply makes a quantitative
definition impossible to sustain. How many rhymes are
allowed in prose? How metrical may it be? We return
finally to typography. Print it as poetry and it is poetry.

In principle, then, prose uses any rhythm it wants, any
rhyme, any pattern of repetition. Prose will not necessarily
be bad because it uses these in combination or frequently. It
will be another kind of prose, demand another attitude. If it
wishes to elicit that attitude explicitly, it will use rhymes
frequently, meter obviously. If it wishes to elicit that
attitude preponderantly, it may elect to use typography to
trigger it. It then becomes poetry. But what was "bad" in
prose does not automatically become "good" in verse. Nor
the other way around. No essential division separates the
two. No one can ever say about any kind of prose, that "this
kind of thing would do very well in poetry, but it is not

suitable for prose." General rules of this sort are nonsense. Prose can be intrinsically "poetic" in courting the pleasures of language as much as poetry, as much as man himself.

Rhythm in prose has long vexed scholars. How rhythmical is this style or that? What effects emerge? How much rhythm ought prose of this sort or that to have? How to describe the rhythm of a prose text? How re-create it? To these add, And how does anyone learn to feel and see the rhythms in prose? For if prose rhythm has been a problem to scholars, to American students it appears a mystification, terra incognita. It is no mystery why. Fowler's usual good sense seized the point immediately (*Modern English Usage*, p. 504): "It is an instinct cultivatable by those on whom nature has not bestowed it, but on one condition only—that they will make a practice of reading aloud." Reading aloud is precisely what no one in America does anymore. To an American university student, the prospect of reading a literary text aloud in class produces a response akin to lockjaw. Reading aloud. An alien activity.

Motives for this paralysis lead us deep into the problem of prose rhythm. Shyness only begins to explain the phenomenon. A reading is a performance. The reader must understand what he performs. To avoid the monotone haste that swallows prose like castor oil, the voice must vary pitch, something Americans find hateful to do. Emphasis must be added, tone considered. The reader, that is, must pick a spirit in which to read. He must choose a relationship with the audience. Sentences must be shaped by the intonation. In long passages, a longer rhythm of thought or argument will emerge, as well as the shorter rhythm of individual sentences. Reading aloud, that is, renders a style, in our sense of the word, opaque. The stylistic surface must be pondered, unavoidably. The sing-song monotone, rhythmical counterpart to the scientific attitude, does not clarify concepts; it obscures them. It does so by boring the reader. A student can be trained to look through a written verbal

surface to the concepts lurking beneath. It is much harder
to ignore a speaking voice. Try reading *Macbeth* in a nasal
monotone.

Rhetorical performance, of course, was what reading
once meant. A Greek or Roman schoolboy did not whiffle
through his assignment at a pace inculcated by Jet-Seed
Dynamic Reading Institute. He first studied it intensively.
He isolated and remarked the figures of speech. He
analyzed the imagery. He studied the shape of a sentence
and devised a speech rhythm to elucidate that shape. He
selected appropriate gestures for significant junctures. He
rehearsed the stages of the argument until the thought
moved with a rhythm of its own. Then he memorized the
passage, rehearsed it a dozen times. He was then ready to
perform it—aloud. Under such a pedagogy, rhythm cannot
be a separate study. It grows naturally from the way the
prose is addressed. A system of rhythm, for example the
series of rhythmic patterns for sentence-closings that the
Middle Ages charted, the *clausulae*, was not planned, but
simply described what the practice of declamation itself
created.

Prose, under such a proceeding, cannot be approached
with the scientific attitude alone. Preoccupation with form,
with the play attitude, is immediate and continual. A
performance is played. The text must be re-created. Surely,
some such pedagogy as this is desperately needed in English
classes in America today. Students are sometimes asked to
memorize a passage of verse. But I have never—Gettysburg
Address to one side—heard of a student being asked to
memorize and declaim a passage of prose. The debater's
training, like Freshman Composition, emphasizes invention, finding arguments, rather than stylistic surface. This is
movement in precisely the wrong direction. And the
speed-reading course is plain lunacy. Its mere premise
horrifies: reading is something to be gotten through. Seldom
has the American dislike and suspicion of words shown so

clearly. Words are to be gotten over with. Mumblespeak *has* to be read this way, of course, but the pattern lingers—you abolish not mumblespeak but humane reading. The ads for such courses always depict a clean-cut young fellow sitting beside a four-foot pile of books, with a caption something like "Bill Herkimer and his Monday's before-breakfast reading." One of the books, I noticed in such an ad, was *Moby Dick*, and another *Paradise Lost*.

Before prose rhythm can be sensibly considered, one must redefine reading. It cannot be a jet flight coast-to-coast. It must be a slow walk in the country, taken, as all such walks should be, partly for the walking itself. Every course in composition ought to be a course in Slow Reading. To read a prose text aloud, again and again, is the most important single act you can perform, if you are to understand its style. As for rhythm, if you do not read aloud (at least with the mind's ear), there will not be any. Rhythm cannot be studied by itself, directly. Until a text is read aloud there is no rhythm to study. Of course we can silent-read for rhythm, but only if we have learned, paradoxically, how to read aloud silently. Until you have explored this dimension of prose style, you will not know it is there. Once you have explored it, you'll find a passage of mumblespeak literally unreadable. With luck, you may not write any more of it yourself.

To consider rhythm, then, you must hear it. To hear it you must read aloud. To read aloud means bringing the play attitude to prose. Thus, to the degree that a prose has rhythm, it will less welcome the play attitude than demand it. It seems no accident that scientific prose, the neutral style, is usually rhythmless, unemphatic, or cacorhythmic. Be consistent enough about prose's not needing rhythm and it will soon have none, as has occurred in America. Pick up a newspaper and try to read it—really read it. The prose will not welcome such attention.

The scholars' difficulty with prose rhythm arises directly

from the situation just described. To hear rhythm you must perform the prose, and no two performances are ever the same. That no two performances of verse are ever the same never seems to enter these discussions, such is the zeal displayed to distinguish prose and verse rhythm on the basis of regularity, of meter. So Professor Saintsbury in his exhaustive and exhausting *History of English Prose Rhythm* (p. 450): "As the essence of verse-metre is its identity (at least in equivalence) and recurrence, so the essence of prose rhythm lies in variety and divergence." And in an earlier encapsulation from the same book (p. 202): "prose and verse rhythm . . . rhythm diverse and rhythm uniform." W. K. Wimsatt points out the contradiction implicit here by remarking that since rhythm implies some kind of regularity, it may not be the best word to use for the patterns of emphasis in prose. In fact, in talking of prose rhythm, scholars sometimes talk nonsense. So Murry, in *The Problem of Style*, writes of the "flexible, non-insistent rhythm that is proper to prose in the pink of condition," the "lithe glancing movement, swiftly and secretly advancing, which is characteristic of prose." But rhythm is insistence, repetition. What else can it be? Rhythm is promise of pattern. Unless you can see the pattern, acknowledge the promise, how can it exist? What are you trying to measure, or at least point to, when you talk of the "rhythm of prose"? What nomenclature do you use to describe whatever it is you are trying to describe?

Kenneth Burke, in his brilliant discussion of prose style in *Counter-Statement* (p. 141), employs a vivid analogy for what the reader experiences as prose rhythm:

The varied rhythms of prose also have their "motor" analogies. A reader sensitive to prose rhythms is like a man running through a crowd; at one time he must halt, at another time he can leap forward; he darts perilously between saunterers; he guards himself in turning sharp corners. We mean that in all rhythmic experiences one's "muscular imagination" is touched. Similarly with sounds, there is some analogy to actual movement, since sounds may rise and fall, and in a remote way one rises and falls with them.

We are trying to describe, then, the movement of a speaking voice. The nomenclature will be that used to describe speech of any sort. The linguists distinguish three fundamental attributes to describe: stress, pitch, and juncture. Stress is simply force, ictus, energy of utterance. Pitch needs no explanation. (To illustrate how language sounds without it, compare an English actor reading Shakespeare with an American one. The American will emphasize by stress, the Englishman far oftener—and far more pleasantly—by changing pitch.) Juncture describes the kinds of connections we make between words. Following a pioneering study by Trager and Smith (*An Outline of English Structure*), four stresses, four pitches, and four junctures may be distinguished. (We might just as easily, of course, distinguish eight, or twelve.)

The stresses: 1) primary (´)
               2) secondary (ˆ)
               3) tertiary (`)
               4) weak (˘)

The pitches: 1) low
               2) middle
               3) high
               4) extra high

The junctures: 1) transitional juncture (+); a regular slight pause between words
               2) fading juncture or caesura (↓) or (#), as at the end of a statement
               3) rising juncture (↑) or (∥); again, as at the end of a statement
               4) sustentional juncture (→) or (|); between two related statements or words (the difference between "night rates" and "nitrates")

Such a simple nomenclature, however inadequate for the

professional linguist, offers many advantages for the beginning student of style. It also escapes a principal disadvantage—it does not force attitudes, it describes. The larger patterns that such an analysis yields are called "intonation patterns," or amalgams of stress, pitch, and juncture. An intonation pattern, then, can depict the trajectory of a voice reading prose. It is intonation on a larger scale. The question intonation, for example (or intonations—there appear to be several), of "What?" is a single voice pattern. You can follow the career longer and describe a pattern. One more variable must be dealt with—time. No absolute units of time can be distinguished; manners and speeds of speech vary. But lengths of time for words and phrases will, whatever the pace, vary one to another. We can thus time a passage as it is read, or suggest a time—work on the actor's "timing," as we say. It should be remembered, obviously, that the unit of timing is not, as it purports to be in metrics, the syllable. We perform a prose text each time we read it, stretching or squeezing together syllables to gain emphasis. We *clarify* it. We elicit from it a movement of voice by no means implicit in the words considered just as a series of syllables. (You need only read a piece of prose as lifelessly as you can, pronouncing clearly and distinctly and with equal stress upon every syllable in it, to see how much even the worst reading adds to a passage, or perhaps we should say, elicits meaning from it.) Rhythm, to call this complex movement of voice by that name, is thus a cooperative venture, created, like clarity, by reader and writer together. A text may support several rhythms with equal justice; one seldom dominates exclusively. Certain rhythms may be suggested, of course, by syntactical habits or word choices. So Samuel Johnson will force a certain kind of ponderous antitheticality upon us, however we read him. But the rhythm of a passage does not simply exist, as does its imagery: reading has to create it.

So from rhythmical prose arises a natural comparison

between rhythm and sense. The sense enters integrally into the performance that creates the rhythm. A writer may choose, or a reader may choose to impose, a rhythm at odds with the sense, thus creating a counterpoint between style and sense. Kingsley Amis has deliciously portrayed such a counterpoint in *Lucky Jim*. The hero is reading the scholarly paper on which his academic future depends. He is drunk. He has kissed the job good-bye and metamorphosed his performance into one that reflects his real feelings.

Gradually, but not as gradually as it seemed to some parts of his brain, he began to infuse his tones with a sarcastic, wounding bitterness. Nobody outside a madhouse, he tried to imply, could take seriously a single phrase of this conjectural, nugatory, deluded, tedious rubbish. Within quite a short time he was contriving to sound like an unusually fanatical nazi trooper in charge of a book-burning reading out to the crowd excerpts from a pamphlet written by a pacifist, Jewish, literate communist. A growing mutter, half amused, half indignant, arose about him, but he closed his ears to it and read on. Almost unconsciously he began to adopt an unnameable foreign accent and to read faster and faster, his head spinning. . . . He began punctuating his discourse with smothered snorts of derision. He read on, spitting out the syllables like curses, leaving mispronunciations, omissions, spoonerisms uncorrected, turning over the pages of his script like a score reader following a *presto* movement, raising his voice higher and higher. At last he found his final paragraph confronting him, stopped, and looked at his audience.

The rich pastures of irony lie open to those who "realize" the rhythm of prose (just as a musical performer "realizes" a text when he fills in the harmony a composer has only sketched). Students of meter often refer to the tension between natural word stress and the stress pattern that meter imposes. In prose rhythm an analogous tension waits there for the exploiting. The reader must supply meaning, color it to a degree that poetry seldom permits. Because of this larger freedom, prose is often more fun to read aloud than poetry.

We must perform prose, and to perform it scan it. The linguists have provided a nomenclature and the use of it, plus literary taste, comes as near a pedagogy for acquiring "an ear for English" as anything today is likely to. Musical notation does not, for various reasons, work well. The perplexities of the standard English metrical system, itself a disastrous leftover from Latin and Greek metrics, confuse far more than enlighten. As illustration we might scan a passage or two. The nomenclature, though hardly perfect, seems more precise than the "easy flow of words" impressionistic guff students, especially beginning students, usually content themselves with.

Here is a passage from Churchill's *History of the Second World War* describing the Battle of Britain. I quote at length. We can dissect a brief passage but need the longer one to feel the style:

We must take September 15 as the culminating date. On this day the Luftwaffe, after two heavy attacks on the 14th, made its greatest concentrated effort in a resumed daylight attack on London.

It was one of the decisive battles of the war, and, like the Battle of Waterloo, it was on a Sunday. I was at Chequers. I had already on several occasions visited the headquarters of Number 11 Fighter Group in order to witness the conduct of an air battle, when not much had happened. However, the weather on this day seemed suitable to the enemy, and accordingly I drove over to Uxbridge and arrived at the Group Headquarters. Number 11 Group comprised no fewer than twenty-five squadrons covering the whole of Essex, Kent, Sussex, and Hampshire, and all the approaches across them to London. Air Vice-Marshal Park had for six months commanded this group, on which our fate largely depended. From the beginning of Dunkirk, all the daylight actions in the South of England had already been conducted by him, and all his arrangements and apparatus had been brought to the highest perfection. My wife and I were taken down to the bomb-proof Operations Room, fifty feet below ground. All the ascendancy of the Hurricanes and Spitfires would have been fruitless but for this system of underground control centres and telephone cables, which had been devised and built before the war by the Air Ministry under Dowding's advice and impulse. Lasting credit is due to all concerned. In the South of England there were at this time Number 11 Group H.Q. and six subordinate fighter station centres. All these were as has been described, under heavy stress. The Supreme Command was exercised from the Fighter Headquarters at Stanmore, but the actual handling of the direction of the squadrons was wisely left to Number 11 Group, which controlled the units through its fighter stations located in each country.

The Group Operations Room was like a small theatre, about sixty feet across, and with two storeys. We took our seats in the dress circle. Below us was the large-scale map-table, around which perhaps twenty highly trained young men and women, with their telephone assistants, were assembled. Opposite to us, covering the entire wall, where the theatre curtain would be, was a gigantic blackboard divided into six columns with electric bulbs, for the six fighter stations, each of their squadrons having a sub-column of its own, and also divided by lateral lines. Thus, the lowest row of bulbs showed as they were lighted the squadrons which were "Standing By" at two minutes' notice, the next row those "At Readiness," five minutes, then "At Available," twenty minutes, then those which had taken off, the next row those which had reported having seen the enemy, the next—with red lights— those which were in action, and the top row those which were returning home.

"I don't know," said Park, as we went down, "whether anything will happen today. At present all is quiet." However, after a quarter of an hour the raid-plotters began to move about. An attack of "40 plus" was reported to be coming from the German stations in the Dieppe area. The bulbs along the bottom of the wall display panel began to glow as various squadrons came to "Stand By." Then in quick succession "20 plus," "40 plus" signals were received, and in another ten minutes it was evident that a serious battle impended. On both sides the air began to fill.

One after another signals came in, "40 plus," "60 plus"; there was even an "80 plus."

Presently the red bulbs showed that the majority of our

squadrons were engaged. A subdued hum arose from the floor, where the busy plotters pushed their discs to and fro in accordance with the swiftly changing situation. Air Vice-Marshal Park gave general directions for the disposition of his fighter force, which were translated into detailed orders to each fighter station by a youngish officer in the centre of the dress circle, at whose side I sat. Some years after I asked his name. He was Lord Willoughby de Broke. (I met him next in 1947, when the Jockey Club, of which he was a steward, invited me to see the Derby. He was surprised that I remembered the occasion.) . . .

The young officer . . . continued to give his orders, in accordance with the general directions of his Group Commander, in a calm, low monotone, and the three reinforcing squadrons were soon absorbed. I became conscious of the anxiety of the Commander, who now stood still behind his subordinate's chair. Hitherto I had watched in silence. I now asked, "What other reserves have we?" "There are none," said Air Vice-Marshal Park. In an account which he wrote about it afterwards, he said that at this I "looked grave." Well I might. What losses should we not suffer if our refuelling planes were caught on the ground by further raids of "40 plus" or "50 plus"! The odds were great; our margins small; the stakes infinite.

Another five minutes passed, and most of our squadrons had now descended to refuel. In many cases our resources could not give them overhead protection. Then it appeared that the enemy were going home. The shifting of the discs on the table below showed a continuous eastward movement of German bombers and fighters. No new attack appeared. In another ten minutes the action was ended. We climbed again the stairways which led to the surface, and almost as we emerged the "All Clear" sounded.

It was 4.30 P.M. before I got back to Chequers, and I immediately went to bed for my afternoon sleep. I must have been tired by the drama of Number 11 Group, for I did not wake till eight. When I rang, John Martin, my principal private secretary, came in with the evening budget of news from all over the world. It was repellent. This had gone wrong here; that had been delayed there; an unsatisfactory answer had been received from so-and-so; there had been bad sinkings in the Atlantic. "However," said Martin, as he finished this account, "all is redeemed

by the air. We have shot down a hundred and eighty-three for a
loss of under forty."

Scanning the opening few lines, first here are the stresses
as they sound to me:

Wĕ mŭst tàke Sĕptèmbèr 15 ás thĕ cûlmĭnătĭng dáte. Ŏn thís dáy
thĕ Lúftwâffĕ, àftèr twò héavȳ ăttâcks ŏn thĕ 14th, mâde îts
gréatĕst cóncentràtèd éffòrt ĭn ă rèsúmed dáylíght ăttáck ŏn
Lóndŏn.
   Ît wâs ône ŏf thĕ dĕcísîve báttlès òf thè wár, ànd, lìke thê Bàttlĕ
ŏf Wâtêrlóo, ĭt wăs ŏn ă Súndáy. Î wàs àt Chéquèrs.

Sir Winston liked stress to fall at the end of sentences. They
close strongly. Context makes dates important. They all
carry primary stress and, because of their force, tend to
weaken and hurry the syllables clustering on either side of
them. If one syllable holds primary stress, the other syllables
of a word are sometimes scarcely pronounced (*London, effort*).
Stress figures so importantly in the passage, in fact, that the
fourfold division seems not flexible enough; eight categories
might be better. "London" probably absorbs twice as much
energy as any other word in the passage. The strong stress at
the end seems a constant, for example, in the second
paragraph: ". . . decisive; . . . war, . . . Waterloo; . . .
Sunday; . . . Chequers." There seems to be a regular
pattern here, several weakly stressed words then a strong
one. Such regularity in prose is presumably to be deplored.
But how regular it will be depends on how regular the
reader makes it. Syllables can be squashed together to
render the pattern more obvious, dwelt upon to make it less
so. The stressed words provide a skeleton: *decisive, war,
Waterloo, Sunday, Chequers.* Around them the reader stands
free, within the basic pattern, to orchestrate stress as he will.
   Will the pitch markings coincide with the stress ones? We
might, as a general rule, expect so.

　　2　　2　　4　　　2　3　　2　　　　　1 2 1　　　2　　2 3　　2 2 2
We must take September 15 (the fifteenth) as the culminating
　1　　1　　　4 3　　　2　4　　1 1　2 2　　2　　1 2　1 1　　　2
date. On this day the Luftwaffe, after two heavy attacks on
2　　　　　　1 1　　　　　　2　2　　　　2 2　　3　2 1 1　1 1
the 14th (fourteenth), made its greatest concentrated effort
2　2　2 2　　　　3 2　　2 3　　2　　1　1
in a resumed daylight attack on London.
　　2　2　2　　2　2 3 3　　3　3 2　2　　3　3
It was one of the decisive battles of the war, and,
3　　　3 3 3 2　　2 2 3　2　2　2 2 2 1　1
like the Battle of Waterloo, it was on a Sunday.
2　　2 2　　　1 1
I was at Chequers.

How much harder pitch is to mark! It depends on personal
speaking habits—and, of course, on whether we speak
English or American. (Listen to Churchill reading one of
his speeches and try to mark it as he reads it.) The stress
and pitch markings seem discrepant. It may be—no one, so
far as I know, has studied it—that the skillful prose writer
hears a constant counterpoint between stress and pitch, and
constantly plays them off against each other. (Hitler, as he
shrieked at the faithful, continually let pitch and stress
coincide. Churchill's counterpoint makes him seem in
control; Hitler's combined stress and emphasis lent him the
hysterical accents of religious ecstasy.) Pitch reinforces
syntax. The simile of Waterloo is set aside as simile by a
consistent rise in pitch. Parenthetical elements often are so
signaled. Pitch supplies the most agile tool for embellish-
ment the reader possesses. Stress often seems undebatable,
but how to govern the pitch of "London"? Here, much
more is left to the reader. When an extraordinary actor—
Paul Scofield for example—reads a passage of prose as good
as this, his pitch changes seem almost a private music, they
open our ears to a performance that even the skillful prose
stylist scarcely suspected.

　　Now for an impression of the junctures:

We (+) must(+) take(+) September(+) (↓) as (+) the(+)
culminating(↑) date.(↓) On(+) this (↑) day(+) the(+) Luft-

waffe,(↓) after(+) two(+) heavy(+) attacks(+) on(+) the(+) 14th, (↑) made(+) its(+) greatest(↑) concentrated(+) effort(+) in(+) a(+) resumed(+) daylight(+) attack(+) on(→) London.(↓)

It(+) was(+) one(+) of(+) the(+) decisive(+) battles(+) of(+) the(+) war, (+) and, (↑) like the Battle of Waterloo, (↓) it(+) was(+) on(+) a(+) Sunday.(↓) I(+) was(+) at(+) Chequers.(↓)

This tells us less than the other two. To really learn something, we should mark only sentence junctures, but do so throughout the whole passage. A larger pattern might then emerge. But Churchill does use juncture skillfully sometimes: "The odds were great( ); our margins small( ); the stakes infinite(→)." Notice, too, how Churchill uses the very short sentence, with change in pitch, for emphatic summary:

I now asked, "What other reserves have we?" "There are none," said Air Vice-Marshal Park. In an account which he wrote about it afterward, he said that at this I "looked grave." Well I might.

Does the voice rise in pitch for the last three words? Fall? Actor's choice. (And who but Churchill would, for the sheer drama of it, give the Air Marshall his full title again, after having earlier used a customary abbreviation?) Or another instance:

I did not wake till eight. When I rang, John Martin, my principal private secretary, came in with the evening budget of news from all over the world. It was repellent.

To feel the larger rhythmic pattern, chart sentence-length in this passage. Not always a precise indicator of rhythm, the pattern of long and short alone often provides the fundamental principle of alternation.

What impressionistic adjective does the analysis call for? *Dramatic* would be my choice. (As befits the scene: "The Group Operations Room was like a small theatre.")

Movement abounds, both in stress and pitch. Keeping the two patterns separate when they naturally want to cohere lends the style authority, puts it in control, in fact, puts it just where Churchill was during the passage—at the center of command. The stress endings generate force. Emphasis falls on the nouns central to the sense. Such prose as this asks to be read aloud. It offers many possibilities for calculated timing, for building a climax, for conveying significance through intonation. One continually feels that English for Churchill was the *spoken* language. His attention to the sound of words never failed. He did not need to think about the rhythm. He heard the words.

Yet our analysis, prolonged into tedium already, hardly conveys a real sense of what Churchill's prose sounds like. The means for describing prose rhythm are still primitive, and the descriptions, like mine above, probably idiosyncratic. If we again become a culture of the spoken word, as the McLuhan thesis expects, those means may grow more luminous. Until then, perhaps we may imply indirectly what has not been rendered directly, the quality of Churchill's prose, by juxtaposing it with a piece of arythmic literary scholarship (Blaze Bonazza, *Shakespeare's Early Comedies*, p. 10):

Attention has been confined here to the earlier comedies with the expectation that a pattern of development would show itself and a final, perfected scheme would become inducible. It is assumed here that Shakespeare did not start out as a fully competent dramatist—that he had to learn this difficult craft gradually, first by tinkering with old plays and collaborating with others. Not until he had worked with the problems of stagecraft as an apprentice did he undertake the fashioning of plays of his own contriving; even then he still relied heavily on imitation. He was still not certain of the path to follow because he had not yet evolved his own concept of the comic and perfected the stage techniques to realize it. He evolved this concept only by working it out in the course of several highly derivative plays in which he tried to master the practical matters of stage techniques, of entrances and exits, of setting up his situation, of initiating complications and conflict, of building suspense to lead to a climactic action, and of unraveling the tangled skein of action he had wound together. It was this process of working his way through these early efforts, of making mistakes and learning from them that made it possible for this highly gifted young poet to learn the difficult art of stagecraft just as Marlowe, endowed with similar gifts, had struggled to learn it but had died before he completely mastered it. Admittedly, these first comedies of Shakespeare, with the exception of *A Midsummer Night's Dream*, are far from the degree of excellence of the best of his later ones. What is primarily held for them is that they show the stages in his progress, uneven as it is, and anticipate the structure of his mature successes in romantic comedy.

Here stress is almost impossible to mark. It varies little. Try to vary pitch and it sounds like silly overdramatizing. The passage has no rhythm, was not written to be spoken, or by one for whom words were *essentially* speech. Sentences run to a similar length—all long. No use is made of the beginnings and endings of sentences, the places of natural stress. The voice falls *naturally* into a monotone. The prose resists performance. The curse of graduate school prose— spelling everything out—lies heavily upon it. Sense often hangs tenuously suspended between grammatically related but geographically distant words: "It was this process . . . [15 words] . . . that made it possible." The strings of parallel prepositional phrases ("of stage techniques, of entrances and exits") beg for some kind of rhythmic arrangement, but none emerges. The prose crawls and the reader sleeps. Such prose not only lacks a speaking voice, it prohibits us from supplying one. Unless prose, and the reading and teaching of prose, regain the habits of speech, we shall all grow equally voiceless.

6   Essential Hypocrisies

The only thing that is indispensable for the possession of a good style is personal sincerity.
                        Sir Herbert Read, *English Prose Style*

Always Be Sincere, whether you mean it or not.
                        Flanders and Swann, "At the Drop of a Hat"

A persistent strand of The Books's moralizing has stressed sincerity in prose composition: Don't put on airs; Write about what you have personally experienced; Try to develop a style of your own. Once again, the sum of such counsel is a text from Polonius. He ends his platitudinous admonitions to his son Laertes with the famous "To thine own self be true." What precedes this ringing phrase, unhappily, is more sensible advice on how to fabricate a safe and expedient self to be true to. Laertes, had he been a bit wittier, could have sensibly replied, "Self?—what self?" So a student might well reply to the preaching of The Books, "How can I be sincere when I haven't yet put together a self to be true to?"

Once again, we surprise an incomplete conception of prose composition. A self is posited, heart-whole, coherent, located somewhere halfway between the ears. It exists. The task is to develop a prose style fully expressive of it. The best style will most closely imitate the unique configurations of this unique self. Notice the similarities to the incomplete argument for clarity discussed earlier. Half the process is left out. Two conceptions of the self have prevailed in the West from the time of the Greeks onward. One we might call the central self, or the soul. To this, the sincerity exhortations are directed. The second depicts the social, dramatic, role-playing self, man as actor not soul. This dramatic self derives its existence from the society surrounding it. How does one remain true to one's social self? What style expresses the inveterate actor and poseur in all of us? What pedagogy can accommodate this shifting self?

Erik Erikson, in his psychoanalytical version of the Seven Ages of Man argument, sees adolescence as a time of role-experiment. A single self has not yet cohered. In this time of identity crisis, first one role is played, then another. Finally a comfortable dramatic creation falls together into a core self. Around this, the dramatic variations continue to play throughout life. Thus the adolescent speaks with literal accuracy of going to college to "find himself." If Erikson's analysis comes close to the mark, traditional "sincerity" pedagogy should be stood on its head. The adolescent stylist should be encouraged to impersonate other people, not "be himself." He should imitate the historical styles until he can live them with ease. He will then feel, and embody, the historical "selves" they express. Every prose style allegorizes a life style. These life styles will become available to an eclectic effort to build a self of one's own. To ask someone to develop a style before he has a self to start from reveals once again The Books' fondness for basing their pedagogy on a vacuum.

The only real stylistic sincerity an adolescent can grasp is a connoisseur's attitude toward language. This stage of selfhood needs, for prose as for life, an exposure to many styles—the more bizarre and self-conscious the better. Traditional pedagogy clamors for the opposite. It insists on a selection of trendy contemporary essays in a neutral expository prose that filters out self. Or we encounter a version of progressive education's "creativity." Here the student gushes. "Right out of the old guts," as Terry Southern put it, "onto the goddam paper." Both strategies premise a self not yet there. The will for it is immensely strong, however. Erikson anatomizes at length the adolescent desire for "rock bottom," for a central orientation or interpretative point of view, a set of spiritual and intellectual coordinates within which a world can be constructed. What pedagogy is demanded here? How can we fit such strong desire for a central norm into the stylistic eclecticism just described? Clearly, normative prose, invisible clarity, defeats this purpose. It cannot express the self, it evaporates it. If real "sincerity" for the student of style means trying to experiment with social selves to find a central one, how can stylistic instruction help?

Such a search is no longer exclusively adolescent. Adulthood for Western man requires just this self-conscious juggling act to hold together the two concepts of self, social and central. A stylistic diagram representing such a tension would go something like this. No single, normative style is forced on us just as, unless we are psychotic, no single self is forced on us. We choose. This choice, always to some extent arbitrary, must build on the fullest survey of possible styles. To speak in a figure, circumference becomes center. "Rock-bottom" is found by charting boundary conditions for expressive style in one's own language. This range of expressivity has limits, however. Thought can express itself only through style. (Some kind of stylization is inevitable, even if only the stylistic act of renouncing style.) And the devices of style are not unlimited. The expressive range of a language works like a jukebox. It can play a great many tunes but not an unlimited number. Individual combinations will be, for practical purposes, unlimited, but not the constitutive elements. Thus "rock-bottom" for stylistic instruction would seem to be a comprehensive survey, as self-conscious as possible, of the basic devices of style available in English. This can be historical or analytical, diachronic or synchronic—it doesn't matter. What it is essential to see is that the quest for "sincerity" leads not to an examination of feelings but to an examination of words. Sincerity begins not in feelings but in sentences.

It follows that a central problem of the composition course—what to write about, what to say—is largely

irrelevant to the search for sincerity. What to say should be
supplied. A range of opinions ought to be furnished and
surveyed along with a range of styles. There is, at rock-bottom, no call for "originality." It ought not to be forced. If a
student hasn't any opinions, let him be given some. Written
utterance, after all, strives for imposture. What is writing's
built-in advantage if not that, in it, we can pretend to be
brighter than we are? Much has been written about prose
that gains authority through the speaking voice. It gains
still more by manipulating time-scale. We condense ten
hours' writing and thinking into one hour's reading. The
best ad-libbers always prepare their spontaneity. Writing's
advantage, as a presentation of self, is not that it allows us to
adopt the mannerisms of speech but that it allows us to
adopt the tempo of speech without its hesitant waste.

If writing is organization of thought, it is also, and by the
same logic, falsification of thought, imposture. (Thus
stream-of-consciousness fictionists, seeking a new style closer
to the real tempo of spontaneous thinking, have to fabricate
a "random" pattern that ends up making some kind of
sense.) Supplying a set of opinions to be presented and
developed as forcefully as possible simply brings into
self-consciousness the coercion that writing always practices
on thought, and hence on us, on our "sincerity." And the
self-consciousness frees us, to the extent that we can be
freed, from that coercion. If we know what puts limits on
our sincerity, what conditions it, we can attain a kind of
sincerity beyond the conditioning. Thus, for prose style, the
way to sincerity lies through verbal artifice, not around it.
Spontaneity, or sincerity, in the composition course, is
largely an affair of manner, not matter.

Again, it follows that the object of study should be the
stylistic surface. Classical treatises of rhetoric, though they
always distinguish the five component parts of oratory, tend
to spend a disproportionate amount of their time on
one—style—and especially on the "figures," the surface

configurations and ornaments of style. Now we can see why. Such a concentration results naturally from the attempt to teach style. Stylistic instruction, therefore, should not try to do away with ornament, it should make love to it. It should attempt to develop a calculus between stylistic and emotional effect. We might instance the pun. The Books deplore it, of course, or allegorize it rather, as an example of language's undependability on the one hand, and its free delights (two meanings from one) on the other.

The study of syntax becomes, in such a calculus, a study in the dynamics of emotional energy. Sincerity will compel us to create, in our sentences' syntax, a model for the emotion we wish to express. The more flexible and inclusive our syntactical and ornamental repertoire, the more "sincere" our prose can become. To describe the full range of such a repertoire has been tried repeatedly in the past. The emphatic effect of euphony and alliteration, the suspensive effect of participles, the nonlogical identities of rhyme, the verb tenses as forms of awareness—these and a hundred more have been cataloged. What is required now is not to ignore this resource but to see in it the building blocks for sincerity in prose.

As a brief example of this kind of stylistic sincerity, consider the two basic stylistic patterns for prose that have been distinguished since the Greeks. They have been called the running style (λέξις εἰρομένη) and the compact or periodic style (λέξις κατεστραμμένη). Here is a fair example of the running style, from Virginia Woolf's *To the Lighthouse* (p. 192):

But what after all is one night? A short space, especially when the darkness dims so soon, and so soon a bird sings, a cock crows, or a faint green quickens, like a turning leaf, in the hollow of the wave. Night, however succeeds to night. The winter holds a pack of them in store and deals them equally, evenly, with indefatigable fingers. They lengthen; they darken. Some of them hold aloft clear planets, plates of brightness. The autumn trees, ravaged as they are, take on the flash of tattered flags kindling in the gloom of cool cathedral caves where gold letters on marble pages describe death in battle and how bones bleach and burn far away in Indian sands. The autumn trees gleam in the yellow moonlight, in the light of harvest moons, the light which mellows the energy of labour, and smooths the stubble, and brings the wave lapping blue to the shore.

Syntax follows sense, either a pattern of association, or of subject, or as here, a chronological sequence. What follows builds upon what went before, modifies it, restates it. A *diachronic* style, we might call it, one that acknowledges the passage of time. It often creates immediacy and action, as in this passage from Fielding's *Shamela* (p. 312), the parodied adventures of a virtuous servant-girl.

O Madam, I have strange things to tell you! As I was reading in that charming book about the dealings, in comes my master—to be sure he is a precious one. Pamela, says he, what book is that? I warrant you Rochester's poems.——No, forsooth, says I, as pertly as I could; why how now saucy chops, boldface, says he—— Mighty pretty words, says I, pert again.——Yes (says he) you are a d--d, impudent, stinking, cursed, confounded jade, and I have a great mind to kick your a--. You, kiss — says I. A-gad, says he, and so I will; with that he caught me in his arms, and kissed me till he made my face all over fire. Now this served purely, you know, to put upon the fool for anger. O! What precious fools men are! And so I flung from him in a mighty rage, and pretended as how I would go out at the door; but when I came to the end of the room, I stood still, and my master cried out, hussy, slut, saucebox, boldface, come hither——Yes, to be sure, says I; why don't you come, says he; what should I come for, says I; if you don't come to me I'll come to you says he; I shan't come to you, I assure you, says I. Upon which he run up, caught me in his arms, and flung me upon a chair, and began to offer to touch my under-petticoat. Sir, says I, you had better not offer to be rude; well, says he, no more I won't then; and away he went out of the room. I was so mad to be sure I could have cried.

Exaggerated movement, this. Slow it down, and you get the gentle flow of historical narrative, as here in this lovely passage from the nineteenth-century *Greville Memoirs* (vol. 5, pp. 160–61):

Death, which has been so busy this year, and striking so indiscriminately, took off a person of a very different description on Sunday last. On that day, after a protracted and painful illness, my uncle's widow, Lady William Bentinck, was released from her sufferings. A more amiable and excellent woman never existed in the world. She was overflowing with affections, sympathies, and kindness, not only perfectly unselfish, but with scrupulous fear, carried to exaggeration, of trespassing upon the ease or convenience of others. Though she had passed all her life in the world, been placed in great situations, and had mingled habitually and familiarly with eminent people, she never was the least elated or spoiled by her prosperity. Her mind was pure, simple, natural, and humble. She was not merely charitable, but was charity itself, not only in relieving and assisting the necessitous, but in always putting the most indulgent constructions on the motives and conduct of others, in a childlike simplicity, in believing the best of everybody, and an incredulity of evil report, which proceeded from a mind itself incapable of doing wrong. . . . Here was one of those rare dispositions which nature had made of its very best materials. She was gentle and cheerful, and, without being clever, was one of those people whom everybody likes, and whose society was universally agreeable, from a certain undefinable charm of sympathy and benevolence which breathed in her, and which was more potent, attractive, and attaching than great talents or extensive information, to neither of which she had any pretension.

The periodic style works differently. It encloses time into a single, syntactically controllable unit, treats experience synchronically rather than diachronically. Here, arrangement controls, not time. In it, order triumphs; in the running style, order operates. The running style surprises the mind operating; in the periodic style, the mind has finished its work. Here is the Great Periodist himself, Samuel Johnson, concluding his *Life of Milton*:

The highest praise of genius is original invention. Milton cannot be said to have contrived the structure of an epic poem, and therefore owes reverence to that vigour and amplitude of mind to which all generations must be indebted for the art of poetical narration, for the texture of the fable, the variation of incidents, the interposition of dialogue, and all the strategems that surprise and enchain attention. But, of all the borrowers from Homer, Milton is perhaps the least indebted. He was naturally a thinker for himself, confident of his own abilities, and disdainful of help or hindrance: he did not refuse admission to the thoughts or images of his predecessors, but he did not seek them. From his contemporaries he neither courted nor received support; there is in his writings nothing by which the pride of other authors might be gratified, or favour gained; no exchange of praise, nor solicitation of support. His great works were performed under discountenance, and in blindness, but difficulties vanished at his touch; he was born for whatever is arduous; and his work is not the greatest of heroic poems, only because it is not the first.

In this style, boundary conditions for the sentence expand. A great deal is arranged in balanced antithesis, parallel, and contrast, and arranged with utmost clarity. Judgment has been pronounced. Process of mind does not show. This style has its narrative echo on a lower order of periodicity. Here is the opening paragraph of S. N. Behrman's biography of Lord Duveen of Millbank (*Duveen*, p. 1):

When Joseph Duveen, the most spectacular art dealer of all time, travelled from one to another of his three galleries, in Paris, New York, and London, his business, including a certain amount of his stock-in-trade, travelled with him. His business was highly personal, and during his absence his establishments dozed. They jumped to attention only upon the kinetic arrival of the Master. Early in life, Duveen—who became Lord Duveen of Millbank before he died in 1939, at the age of sixty-nine—noticed that Europe had plenty of art and America had plenty of money, and his entire astonishing career was the product of that simple observation. Beginning in 1886, when he was seventeen, he was perpetually journeying between Europe, where he stocked up, and America; where he sold. In later years, his annual itinerary was relatively fixed: At the end of May, he would leave New York for London, where he spent June and July; then he would go to Paris for a week or two; from there he would go to Vittel, a health resort in the Vosges Mountains, where he took a three-week cure; from Vittel he would return to Paris for another fortnight; after that, he would go back to London; some time in September, he would set sail for New York, where he stayed through the winter and early spring.

This is the same *kind* of style Johnson uses, but the corners are softened, habits varied. The word περίοδος in Greek meant a going-around, a circuit, and thus came to mean a well-rounded sentence, an extensive survey, and one with shape. The periodic style, then, may represent pattern, and the running style, process.

A nomenclature has been built on this fundamental division, and subcategories spun off it. But other nomenclatures could be devised, departing from other antithetical comparisons or tripartite divisions. Grammatical categories could function as a terminology. We might have the simple-sentence style, as illustrated by Hemingway, the compound-complex, as in the later Henry James, or, as with Faulkner, an ever-mutating combination. These categories refer to grammar only; the period-running distinction, to sense, syntax, and rhythm. The most common descriptions of styles refer to effect on the reader, a terminology of impression. The mind of the beholder is described, not the style itself: "racy," "flip," "informal." A famous linguist (Bally) defined style as the force *parole* exerts on *langue*. (*Langue* is the inherited capability of a language, *parole* the use an individual makes of it, the reality he wrings from potentiality.) Apply this definition of style, and the impressionistic terminology seems a necessity, since the *parole* is a category unto itself, unique, available to description only through the unique particularity of defining metaphor.

A sentence, then, has sound, shape, and significance. Just

as there is no canonical formula for the relationship of the three, there is no canonical formula for *describing* the relationship among the three. How many types of prose style are there? Two or more, depending on what categories are selected. I suggested earlier a criterion of self-consciousness. Other reader-writer criteria might develop from this: a relationship of authority (Christ's teaching in the Gospels); a bargaining relationship, the rhetorical contest of the marketplace; a supplication, as in prayer. Descriptive definitions of style are potentially numerous. Which is used—or invoked— seems less important than the stylistic self-consciousness that comes from applying one.

The Books, then, offer a simplistic conception of sincerity in prose because they proceed from a simplistic conception of self. If the central self is established through a pattern of experimentation with social or dramatic selves—with roles —then sincerity in prose will have to follow a similar pattern and find a central style by playing at, and with, a great many styles. And the two processes will influence one another. To play with styles is to play with roles, with ways of thinking and, thus, ways of being. Prose style is always a presentation of self. Its pedagogy ought, therefore, to follow what we know about the formation of self. Style is indeed, as Buffon most famously said, the man himself—but the man sometimes as he is, sometimes as he wants to be, sometimes as he is palpably pretending to be, sometimes, as in comedy, both as he pretends to be and as he is. Stylistic pedagogy ought to cover the whole range. Only by doing so can it perform its authentic social duty: to enhance both clear communication between citizens and the selfhood of the citizens who are communicating.

7   The Ultimate Morality of Mind

The style is the man. Rather say the style is the way the man takes himself. . . . If it is with outer seriousness, it must be with inner humor. If it is with outer humor, it must be with inner seriousness.

Robert Frost, *Letters*

As philosophic counterpart to the American pedagogy of clarity, a very high seriousness toward the cultural role of language has emerged. Every prophet of doom, when chronicling our national descent down the rat-hole of his choice, deplores the current state of our language. So Jacques Barzun, in his brilliant and witty *The House of Intellect*, warns us that "The state of the mother tongue is in fact the index of our control over destiny." And the current state is, of course, grotesque. Barzun poses the problem fairly. Language reveals national psychoses but does not necessarily cause them. Most have not been so cautious. For them, language is usually the cause, the villain. Solve the prose problem—If Everyone Would Only Be Clear—and the rest will fade away. Inasmuch as this varies St. Thomas More's, "All things will not be well until all men are good—Which I do not think will be Lo! these many long years," no one can quarrel with it. Any causal connection more particular than this has never been proven. Prophets who wish people would be clearer really, like Barzun, wish they would be a little brighter. Again, no one can quarrel with this.

But the proposition that we are worse off than earlier times or countries abides no proof. We cannot go back and test or control enough variables. And of course—the problem of infinite regress—we have to use language to talk about language. The whole question, put in these terms, becomes futile. We are, as I said earlier, the only country ever prosperous and democratic enough to *have* a prose problem. This book has argued that we need a new theory and pedagogy of prose style to meet a new problem. The old crackpot utilitarianism won't work. If changes in language or language instruction can change the fate of nations, we're the first country in a position to do anything about it. There are, then, two questions. Does instruction in language make any difference for our future? And is that linguistic future really so desperate as it seems? The preceding chapters have suggested answers to the first question. Before reviewing them, let me put the case for desperation as strongly as possible and see what can be said about it.

Failure to pay the costs of mass education has given the schools chronic intellectual heart trouble for most of this century, and the universities now follow suit. Few care to write well and fewer know how. The media bombardment converts us into, if not McLuhan's global village, at least something unexpected. Our national conversation resembles a spastics' convention where everyone says "You know?" and nobody knows. Our political utterance is congested with what my research assistant, in an inspired typographical error, rendered as "Eisenhoweverese." Our sentimental mass democracy denies the very idea of standards. Everybody just lets it all hang out. We reduce ourselves to machines with an electronic slang of "plugged-in" and "turned-on." The New Left, like the Hitler Right, addicts itself to tantrum prose. We are suffering from a ludicrous case of national euphemism.

Atop all this, twirling its dark moustache, sits the real villain, advertising. Here are two truly wise men on the subject. First, Northrop Frye (*The Well-Tempered Critic*, p. 46):

The mob's version of the high style is advertising, the verbal art of penetrating the mind by prodding the reflexes of the ego. As long as society retains any freedom, such advertising may be largely harmless, because everybody knows that it is only a kind of ironic game. As soon as society loses its freedom, mob high style is taken over by the new masters, to become what is usually called propaganda. Both advertising and propaganda, however, represent the conscious or unconscious pressure on a genuine society to force it into a mass society, which can only be done by debasing the arts.

We're flooded, then, with mob style. George F. Kennan ranks it as a danger just behind war and pollution (*Democracy and the Student Left*, pp. 230–32):

Next to it [ecology] I would have to put something that will surprise most people—something that many people, in fact, will fail utterly to understand. This is the phenomenon of American advertising, and the extent to which it has been permitted to dominate and exploit the entire process of public communication in our country. It is to me positively inconceivable that the whole great, infinitely responsible function of mass communication, including very important phases of the educational process, should be farmed out—as something to be mined for whatever profit there may be in it—to people whose function and responsibility have nothing to do with the truth—whose function and responsibility, in fact, are concerned with the peddling of what is, by definition, untruth, and the peddling of it in trivial, inane forms that are positively debauching in their effect on the human understanding. After the heedless destruction of natural environment, I regard this—not advertising as such, but the consignment to the advertiser of the entire mass communications process, as a concession to be exploited by it for commercial gain—as probably the greatest evil of our natural life. We will not, I think, have a healthy intellectual climate in this country, a successful system of education, a sound press, or a proper vitality of artistic and recreational life, until advertising is rigorously separated from every form of legitimate cultural and intellectual communication—until advertisements are removed from every printed page containing material that has claim to intellectual or artistic integrity and from every television or radio program that

has these same pretensions, from every roadside and every bit of
countryside that purports to offer to the traveler a glimpse of what
his continent once was and once again might be.

The media, the only agency that can educate in a mass
society, have been whored out for profit. The power that
should educate the imagination instead brutalizes it. The
media, advertising especially, cultivate inattention as a
habit, an ingrained pattern of reading and seeing. Though
it holds repetition a premise, the ad is a one-time experience. Advertising repels wonder. It degrades willing suspen-
sion of disbelief into perpetual cynical suspicion. Advertising uses up language; a thousand novels could not wear it
out so fast. Advertising pollutes language.

The palpable falsity of advertising continually reinforces
a view of language as the father of lies. Daniel Boorstin has
written eloquently on the falsity of American life, its
dominant pseudo quality (*The Image: A Guide to Pseudo-Events
in America*, 1964). Advertising language is pseudo language,
creating the substance it pretends to describe. One recent
widely publicized study showed that even three- and
four-year-old children had developed a full-fledged suspicion of ads, and hence of language. A kind of depraved
poetry, it invents an "image" which, unlike the products
bought in its name, retreats before us like a mirage.

End of Case for Desperation. It's a powerful one. But is it
fair to how we stand now? Doesn't it ignore the enormous
hunger for style and stylistic play now abroad in America?
This urge to stylize overwhelms anyone who walks around
an American campus. Wild eclecticism of dress, public
love-making, consciously exaggerated addiction to slang,
robust bearding of the bourgeois—all testify to a hunger for
style. Even the widespread dissatisfaction with the quality of
instruction may stem from the styleless democracy of
prevailing student-professor relationships. The whole university scene, as the *institution* creates it, apotheosizes drab,

offers the student no opportunity to play the student formally. Hunger for style may explain the contribution that blacks are making to the American campus. Rich in style, their slang now seems destined to capture the straight culture as it captured the hippie one. Raw, brutal, intensely metaphorical, it feeds the hungers that scientific prose starves. Since nobody has trained them in the scientific attitude, black Americans have never lost the sense of play with words.

We find around us, then, both intense stylization (and its superficial symptom, faddishness) and intense hunger for style—especially for style in behavior, for drama. (Much of the sit-in phenomenon can be traced to adolescents' hunger to dramatize their roles as students, to dramatize feelings balked of public manifestation.) To feel fully you must feel publicly. You must stylize your feelings. Thus happenings and participatory theater. It is even possible to subsume one of the most unsavory of the recent campus phenomena, the Free and Filthy Speech movements, under the rubric of stylistic hunger. Foul language seems to satisfy a degraded hunger for sacramental speech, for a language at its least transparent and utilitarian.

We might even find in the full sacramental speech of America—advertising—signs of the play-spirit. The crosstalk between ads (VW, Hertz, Avis), the frequent punning and verbal play, the TV commercials grown into minidramas that appeal, increasingly, through style. Dishonest though it be, might not advertising depart from premises more honest than those marshaled by the pedagogy of clarity and closer to the real nature of human motive? Advertising causes people to mistrust language, but might it not also be teaching people to enjoy it? The picture of the young child singing an ad cliché to himself fills us with loathing. We'd prefer him to be rehearsing "Shall I compare thee to a summer's day." But isn't the enjoyment of language rather like reading? It's a habit. What dif-

ference if it's trash that gets you in the habit? Language in
advertising is at least always visible. It is not argued out of
existence. And it is full of affect, of feeling, of desire. Feeling
and color. Opaque. If it is the poetry of the poor—and in
the life of the imagination most of America is poor—it is
certainly bad poetry. But isn't this better than none?
Nothing is what it replaces. If the state of our mother
tongue can be sustained and embellished only by a people
self-conscious about language, advertising may do more to
engender this self-consciousness than the transparent, denotative prose that ignores language to wait exclusively on
meaning.

A few other signs hint that we are becoming self-conscious, or style-conscious, about our language. The most
obvious looms so large we tend to ignore it—the composition crisis itself. We may meet it with the wrong strategy,
but that we want to meet it at all argues a high level of
awareness. We're plagued by jargon, but as we've seen,
people now counter by playing with it. Black idiom is
played at by the stylistically deprived upper-middle class.
The minorities have developed a proud self-consciousness
about their own languages and speak them symbolically.
Even the Webster's Third outcry—too many colloquialisms
accepted as standard—may fit here. People were upset
because The Great Game of Correct Usage seemed about to
fold its tents. Needless fear—a game so pleasant as correctness will be reinvented spontaneously.

Such stylistic self-consciousness makes sense. American
society as a whole is going this way. Increasingly self-conscious about economy, ethics, structure of self, why should
we not be about language? A mass society now reenacts the
aristocratic Renaissance discovery that man's nature is
artifice. Our present concern with pseudo event and our
craving for spontaneity testify to a wide shouldering of the
Renaissance burden. De Tocqueville predicted—truly as
usual—that American writing would ignore niceties of style

and decorum, aristocratic elegance. Don't the signs now suggest an aristocratic stage beyond the utilitarian one? We certainly possess the only begetter of aristocratic taste, moneyed leisure. In the future that Alvin Toffler has conjured up in *Future Shock,* utilitarian pressure will evaporate entirely. We won't have to do anything. Everything will be done for pleasure. The proud slogans of the Renaissance will become literally true. Man will remake himself in whatever form or style he chooses. We shall have to develop both acute self-consciousness and an equally acute sense of style. Electronic intelligence may entirely appropriate prose's obligation to communicate concepts. Such a world speaks and writes entirely for pleasure, entirely for style. The Books' ideal stylist may find himself endowed, in de Maupassant's phrase, "with a perspicacity which strongly resembles incompetence."

The spastic present, then, does not lack signs of hope. We may come to think of our verbal environment as we are learning to think of our physical environment, as something to be cultivated and cherished, not taken for granted. Assuming this to be so, what benefits might accrue? Beyond its self-liquidating help in communicating concept, is prose style good for anything?

We've rehearsed some answers already. A style can serve as paradigm for a social role, an identity. Modern personality theory suggests that we all have many personalities, many selves among whom we choose as occasion requires. Many styles, many selves—which style is which man? Buffon's maxim proves more serviceable when inverted. The man?—he is the style itself. A good style can *create* a personality. When he finds it does so consistently, the writer will name it, as Samuel Clemens named Mark Twain. Flaubert called style "une manière de voir," a way of seeing. We might call it a way of behaving. We have arrived at life style, the shape we give our lives. A style, thought of in this way, might seem much like a psychological experiment—a set of boundary conditions within which meaningful answers can be found. Our language sets limits to what we can know and feel. Speak a different language, inhabit a different universe. Style might be viewed as imposing, on a smaller scale, limits to what we can know and how we can feel. On a yet smaller scale, a literary style sets limits to our expectations, to what kinds of experience we look forward to. It creates a closed universe of discourse.

Stylistic awareness, then, makes possible dialogue with ourselves. It may serve the community as much by enriching the communicator as by clarifying the communication. As clearly, it will empower us to enter into the past, look through lost eyes, participate in the past's way of seeing and thus enrich our own. The study of prose styles serves to introduce, too, a keen self-consciousness about human perception and knowledge. It thus fits neatly into what Daniel Bell and others have seen as the informing principle of the new undergraduate university curriculum—the study of method. Style as visible, self-conscious, opaque, forms part of a curriculum whose center will be self-consciousness, whose rock-bottom is an awareness of boundary conditions. The worship of clarity, like the Newtonian concept of matter and the nineteenth-century historian's concept of fact, becomes part of a larger pattern of larger truth. The stylistic spectrum developed in chapter 3 thus makes sense in terms of, indeed emerges from, a new and promising conception of the undergraduate curriculum.

"In its simplest manifestation," Kenneth Burke maintains, "style is ingratiation" (*Permanence and Change*, p. 50). This leads us down the road opposite from Buffon, from the individual toward society. By a sense of style we socialize ourselves. Style finally becomes, as Burke works it out, social custom (pp. 346–47, n. 1):

Style is a constant meeting of obligations, a state-of-being-without offense, a repeated doing of the "right" thing. It moulds our actions by contingencies, but the contingencies go to the farthest reaches of the communicative. For style (custom) is a complex scheme of what-goes-with-what, carried through all the subtleties of manner and attitude. Its ample practice in social relationships can take the place of competitive success because it is success.

Style defines situations, tells us how to act in them. A prose style defines a literary situation. We return to our emphasis on the self-consciousness shared by writer and reader. In society, it is called manners, in literature, decorum. Style as personality implies an agonistic relationship, a contest. We must feel the force of this great man, like it or not. By his style as by his presence, we are to be overpowered. But style as ingratiation offers an alternative to competition. It aims at the gentlest kind of persuasion, the attempt to make oneself over in the form most agreeable to the other. The study of prose style reveals its most immediate social applicability viewed under such a definition. For literary decorum can function—probably does, used in this way or not—as a model for social decorum. Value judgments, under such a definition, cannot be absolute. If you say, style being ingratiation, that a style has value independent of its audience, you really posit a certain kind of audience as correct. You are, in effect, making a statement about the trainability of a certain kind of audience. Style, in such a definition, is an orchestration of probable acceptances. If they don't work, it's a bad style.

We move easily from style as ingratiation to Whitehead's drumroll, "Style is the ultimate morality of mind" (*Aims of Education*, p. 24). We might argue that the underpinning of morality, the feeling for right behavior, is as much aesthetic as moral judgment. Prose style exercises, and can exorcise too, our range of possible behavior. By allowing the luxury of imaginative rehearsal, it confers real ethical choice, and to this extent frees us from necessity. Ethics at this point touches taste, indeed becomes it.

The study of style constitutes for man an intrinsically satirical, a fundamentally comic pursuit. A style, as Schopenhauer said, is a mask. Stylistic study, by the logic of its address, unmasks us. It teaches us that there is nothing inevitable about our self, or selves, our thoughts, or the words they are clothed in. It demonstrates how much thought sometimes owes to styles and, sometimes, how little. It recapitulates the whole range of human dependence on words. Above all, the study of verbal style is radically reductive of motive. It satirizes high seriousness. The art of translation that any teacher performs when he corrects a paper is essentially satirical. He is ridiculing pretense, revealing a simplified and usually demeaning reality behind it. This satire a student must learn to perpetrate on his own prose and his own self. Both yield the same comic awareness of self and the limitations of self. And such comic self-awareness is, of course, the central requirement for the citizen of a self-conscious society. To know that we are mistaken, and necessarily so, is the art of spiritual openness and welcome that makes such a society possible.

Above all, what we learn about ourselves from study of the whole stylistic spectrum is the inevitable self-pleasing ingredient in all human behavior. When we have restricted clarity, the desire to speak plainly, to its proper small segment of the spectrum, we soon come to know that, in the broad range that is left, we entertain concepts because concepts entertain us. Such awareness does not rule out altruistic motive, but it does prevent flattering overestimations. Just as Hamlet discovers that the deepest motive for his own behavior is not revenge but acting the revenge hero, the pleasures of acting for its own sake, so we learn that beneath all our pleas for clarity and expressivity runs a substratum of verbal play. Motive has always been the question of questions for Freshman Composition. Perhaps more success might flow from assuming, paradoxically, that the deepest motive for writing is not communication at all but the pleasures of writing for its own sake. Writing to others is a writing for ourselves. Clarity in communication may be less the cause of our pleasure in prose than the result.

Bibliographical Note

Freshman Composition texts abound beyond enumeration here—and perhaps anywhere. Readers interested in their development—or lack of it—might be well served by comparing a sampling of current texts with earlier ones. For the language in the national life, the beginning study is Noah Webster, *Dissertations on the English Language* (Boston, 1789; reprinted Gainesville, Fla., with an introduction by Harry R. Warfel, 1951). The most complete, and in many ways the most thoughtful, nineteenth-century text is Alexander Bain's *English Composition and Rhetoric*, 2 vols. (New York, 1888). Bain is especially thorough on the emotional effects of verbal ornamentation. The current form of The Books seems to have come of age around 1900. See, as examples: Austin Phelps and Henry Allyn Frink, *Rhetoric: Its Theory and Practice* (New York, 1895); George Herbert Palmer, *Self-Cultivation in English* (1897); A. M. Wisely, *A New English Grammar* (1898); John Franklin Genung, *The Working Principles of Rhetoric* (1900). As for twentieth-century textbooks, perhaps a brief representative sampling may serve as starting point for further investigation:

James Bradstreet Greenough and George Lyman Kittredge, *Words and Their Ways in English Speech* (1901)

Robert Waters, *The English Grammar of William Cobbett, in a series of letters addressed to his son* (1901)

Hammond Lamont, *English Composition* (1906)

Robert Herrick, *Composition and Rhetoric, for Schools* (1908)

Sterling Andrus Leonard, *English Composition as a Social Problem* (1917)

H. Robinson Shipherd, *The Fine Art of Writing, for Those Who Teach It* (1926)

Burges Johnson, *Written Composition in American Colleges* (1936)

Harold F. Graves, *Types of Persuasion* (1938)

Donald Davidson, *American Composition and Rhetoric* (1939)

John C. Hodges, *Harbrace College Handbook* (1941)

Cleanth Brooks and Robert Penn Warren, *Modern Rhetoric* (1949)

James M. McCrimmon, *Writing with a Purpose* (1950)

George S. Wykoff and Harry Shaw, *The Harper Handbook of College Composition* (1952)

Robert Hamilton Moore, *Effective Writing* (1955)

Donald J. Lloyd and Harry R. Warfel, *American English in its Cultural Setting* (1956)

Harold C. Martin, *The Logic and Rhetoric of Exposition* (1957)

Richard E. Hughes and P. Albert Duhamel, *Rhetoric, Principles and Usage* (1962)

Edward P. J. Corbett, *Classical Rhetoric for the Modern Student* (1965)

Sheridan Baker, *The Complete Stylist* (1966)

John M. Kierzek and Walter Gibson, *The Macmillan Handbook of English* (1966)

Robert W. Daniel, *A Contemporary Rhetoric* (1967)

William Schwab, *Guide to Modern Grammar and Exposition* (1967)

Alan H. Vrooman, *Good Writing: An Informal Manual of Style* (1967)

Richard M. Eastman, *Style* (1970)

Roger Sale, *On Writing* (1970)

Virginia Tufte, *Grammar as Style* (1971)

James E. Miller, Jr., *Word, Self, Reality* (1972)

Rudolf Flesch, *Say What You Mean* (1973)

For more modern scholarly discussions of prose style, see J. Middleton Murry, *The Problem of Style* (Oxford, 1922); Bonamy Dobree, *Modern Prose Style* (Oxford, 1937); James R. Sutherland, *On English Prose* (Toronto, 1937); Herbert Read, *English Prose Style* (London, 1963). Murry is much the most thoughtful of the four, but all preach the gospel of normative clarity. A more recent survey of style and recent thinking about it is Graham Hough's *Style and Stylistics* (London, 1969). This provides a very sensible and commendably brief introduction to the current study of style. A considerably longer and much more ambitious book is James L. Kinneavy's *A Theory of Discourse* (Englewood Cliffs, N.J., 1971). In setting forth his theory, Kinneavy surveys practically every other theory, classical and modern. The bibliographies are especially useful. Longer bibliographies, especially of more recent sylistic study, are: Richard W. Bailey and Dolores M. Burton, *English Stylistics: A Bibliography* (Cambridge, Mass., 1967); Louis T. Milic, *Style and Stylistics: An Analytical Bibliography* (New York, 1967); Helmut Hatzfield, *A Critical Bibliography of the New Stylistics Applied to the Romance Literatures, 1900–1952* and *1953–65* (Chapel Hill, 1953 and 1966).

On the pedagogy of style, Jacques Barzun has many sensible things to say in *Teacher in America* (New York, 1945). On the place of stylistic study in modern pedagogy, readers following the standard pedagogy bibliographies might not come across the recurrent excellent discussions in Alfred North Whitehead's *The Aims of Education* (New York, 1924). Many of the philosophical and pedagogical problems touched on in the foregoing chapters received their first full modern discussion in John Henry Cardinal Newman's *The Idea of a University* (1853–58). An interesting study by a political scientist, Robert F. Lane, *The Liberties of Wit* (New Haven, 1961), considers the civic consequences of the literary emphasis on style rather than verifiable conceptual content. A conservative view of the modern academic atmosphere and its implications for stylistic study is presented in Jacques Barzun's *The House of Intellect* (New York, 1954); a liberal view, in Neil Postman and Charles Weingartner's *Teaching as a Subversive Activity* (New York, 1969).

For comprehensive collections of comment on style by both the famous and the forgotten, consult: William T.

Brewster's *Representative Essays on the Theory of Style* (London, 1921); H. Robinson Shipherd, *The Fine Art of Writing* (New York, 1926); Rollo W. Brown, *The Writer's Art, by Those Who Have Practiced It* (Cambridge, Mass., 1921); Louis T. Milic, *Stylists on Style* (New York, 1969); Leonard Dean and Kenneth G. Wilson, *Essays on Language and Usage*, 2nd ed. (New York, 1963); Howard S. Babb, *Essays in Stylistic Analysis* (New York, 1972). Examples of recent work in the overlapping areas of semantics, linguistics, and literary style can be found in *Style in Language* [ed. Thomas A. Sebook] (Cambridge, Mass., 1960); *Literary Style: A Symposium* [ed. Seymour Chatman] (London, 1971). An especially interesting collection of papers by a single hand is Stephen Ullman's *Language and Style* (Oxford, 1964).

Modern defenses of ornament in prose are hard to come by. Thomas De Quincey's "Style" is a nineteenth-century *locus classicus* (reprinted in *Selected Essays on Rhetoric by Thomas De Quincey*, ed. Frederick Burwick [Carbondale, Ill., 1967]); Walter Pater's "Style" (reprinted in the Brewster collection cited above), and Logan Pearsall Smith's gallant rearguard action, "Fine Writing" (*Society for the Preservation of English*, Tract no. 46, [Oxford, 1936]) both argue the case for ornament. The terms used to catalog verbal ornament have been arranged both alphabetically and by type in my *A Handlist of Rhetorical Terms* (Berkeley and Los Angeles, 1969). Discussion of ornamental style occurs passim under various entries there, and a bibliography of Classical and Renaissance rhetorical treatises is included.

The issues raised by the dogma of clarity in prose can be pursued in several directions. I. A. Richards has proposed a tripartite division of language in some ways analogous to the three attitudes distinguished in the previous chapters. See *Principles of Literary Criticism* (London, 1925); *The Philosophy of Rhetoric* (Oxford, 1936); and, with C. K. Ogden, *The Meaning of Meaning* (1923). The relationship between scientific and intuitive thinking has been explored by

Jerome S. Brunner in *The Process of Education* (New York, 1960) and *On Knowing* (Cambridge, Mass., 1960). Thomas S. Kuhn's *The Structure of Scientific Revolutions* (International Encyclopedia of Unified Science, vol. 2, no. 2 [Chicago, 1962]) is immensely suggestive for the consideration of prose styles as separate paradigms, closed orientations, or systems of value. His discussion of "inter-paradigm debate" really provides the best model currently available for evaluative comparison of different styles. On the outdated scientific theories underlying the dogma of clarity, see Michael Polanyi's *Personal Knowledge* (Chicago, 1958). Much of his book considers, though not under this rubric, the stylistic component of scientific knowing.

The role of the perceiver can be followed in a number of directions. Ernst Cassirer built his philosophy of symbolic forms on the conception of language as a symbolic reality, something man both conceives and perceives. Man's reality, he argues in *An Essay on Man* (New Haven, 1949), is a symbolic one of his own making, not a preexistent one "out there." Thus one can read his *The Logic of the Humanities* (trans. Clarence S. Howe, New Haven, 1960) as an attack on the very conception of reality The Books' dogma of clarity is built upon. Owen Barfield attacks this "scientific" conception of reality in *Saving the Appearances* (London, 1957), a brilliant plea for a kind of knowing that allows man to participate in reality—to create it rather than simply observe it. The implications of such a humanistic or mythical theory of knowledge are treated in J. Bronowski's *Science and Human Values* (New York, 1956). The same author's *The Identity of Man* (New York, 1965) explores the interrelations of theory of knowledge and theory of self, as well as, in a brilliant chapter titled "The Machinery of Nature," dealing with the imaginative or stylistic ingredient in scientific knowing.

The role of the perceiver in art has been dealt with in E. H. Gombrich's famous *Art and Illusion* (New York, 1961), a book that manages to grow from an art history focus into a treatment, first of perception in all art, and then of perception itself. Gombrich shows that what we see depends both on what we expect to see and on the frame we have been taught to see it in and with. His conclusions carry the most profound implications for normative doctrines of prose style. So, too, does Morse Peckham's exciting study of art in terms of the perceiver's role, *Man's Rage for Chaos* (New York, 1965). Peckham considers art to be not a class of objects but a pattern of expectations in the reader. Here is a theoretical underpinning for the attitudes toward prose developed in the previous chapters. Peckham's theory of art contends that the dynamic operation worked on the observer is finally not an ordering but a disordering one. Again, the implication would be that a normative theory of prose style no longer possesses any theoretical basis.

The use of the dramatic metaphor to describe both self and society has been most profoundly argued in our time by Kenneth Burke, especially in *The Philosophy of Literary Form* (2d ed., Baton Rouge, La., 1967) and *Permanence and Change* (1935). His idea of style as essentially a way of seeing, a world view or orientation, rather than something seen through, provides the theoretical basis for any philosophical conception of style in our time. His continual effort to move from verbal style to life style, to avoid the unthinking, neutral descriptions of verbal configurations that have so plagued discussions of style, has opened the way to a great deal of thinking about role-playing by social scientists. Readers interested in the idea of self as role might find the writings of the sociologist Erving Goffman of interest, especially *The Presentation of Self in Everyday Life* (New York, 1959). Wylie Sypher has written eloquently of *Loss of the Self in Modern Literature and Art* (New York, 1962). And Charles Fair has explored the relation of the two conceptions of self, social and central, in both a physiological and a historical context, in his pessimistic but persuasive *The Dying Self*

(Middletown, Conn., 1969). The writings of R. D. Laing, too, have explored the dynamics of the self; see especially *The Divided Self* (London, 1959). Erik H. Erikson's views on the growth of the human personality are set forth in his *Childhood and Society* (rev. ed., 1964). A fascinating historical application is made in *Young Man Luther* (1958).

Readers interested in the concept of play and the aesthetic or game model for motive will find Johan Huizinga's *Homo Ludens* (London, 1949) of great interest. For a genetic, rather than a historical, analysis, see Jean Piaget's *Play, Dreams and Imitation in Childhood* (trans. C. Gattegno and F. M. Hodgson, New York, 1951).

J. A. C. Brown has provided a sensibly cynical assessment of the force the media exert upon us in *Techniques of Persuasion* (1963). His hard-nosed conclusion is that people are less persuadable than we think. If someone is seriously deluded by the media, there must have been something wrong with him to begin with.

The most stimulating discussion of the relation of syntax to emotional response remains, it seems to me, the "Lexicon Rhetoricae" section of Kenneth Burke's *Counter-Statement* (New York, 1931). Burke's philosophical discussion of verbal ornament as metaphor for motive in *A Rhetoric of Motives* (Berkeley and Los Angeles, 1969) remains, too, the most wide-ranging consideration of the implications of verbal ornament. Of the philosophical implications of the neutral style in prose, Roland Barthes's *Writing Degree Zero* (Boston, 1970) constitutes a most provocative modern statement.